D1825921

Grammar Springboards

The fun teaching resource that enables children
to jump ahead in grammar

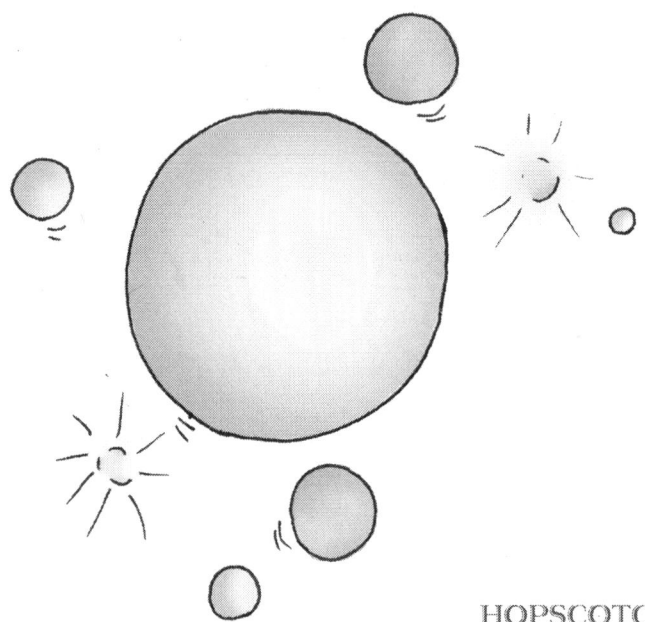

Alison Milford

HOPSCOTCH

A division of MA Education Ltd

HOPSCOTCH

Published by
Hopscotch, a division of MA Education,
St Jude's Church, Dulwich Road, London,
SE24 0PB
www.hopscotchbooks.com
020 7738 5454

©2010 MA Education Ltd.

Written by Alison Milford

Illustrated by Emma Turner,
Fonthill Creative, 01722 717057

ISBN 978 1 90539 074 8

Contents

Introduction   6

Literacy learning objectives   8
reference chart

Chapter 1 – Nouns
Nouns information   11
Noun Springboards   12
Lesson plans and activities:
- Common nouns   13
- Proper nouns   18
- Compound nouns   23
- Plural nouns ending with 's'   27
- Articles - 'an' and 'a'   32

Chapter 2 Pronouns
Pronouns information   36
Pronoun Springboards   37
Lesson plans and activities:
- Pronouns for single nouns   38
- Pronouns for plural nouns   43

Chapter 3 Verbs
Verbs information   50
Verb Springboards   51
Lesson plans and activities:
- Action verbs   52
- Saying verbs   57
- Simple past tense verbs ending with 'ed' or 'd'   63
- Simple present tense verbs ending with '-ing'   68
- Irregular verbs   74

Chapter 4 –Adjectives
Adjectives information   81
Adjective Springboards   83
Lesson plans and activities:
- Descriptive adjectives 1 - settings   84
- Descriptive adjectives 2 - characters   88
- Antonym adjectives   94
- Synonym adjectives   99

Chapter 5 -Making sentences
Sentences information   105
Sentence Springboards   106
Lesson plans and activities:
- Simple sentences   107
- Compound sentences - conjunctions   112
- Time connectives   117
- Prepositions   123

Chapter 6- Punctuation
Punctuation information   128
Punctuation Springboards   129
Lesson plans and activities:
- Questions   130
- Commas in lists   136
- Speech marks   143

Assessments   147
Periodic Assessment tests (Two levelled tests)   148
Transitional Assessment tests (Two levelled tests)   172
Assessment reference charts
- Writing Assessment chart   185
- Reading Assessment chart   187

CD-ROM

Lesson resources

Worksheets
(Two levelled worsheets per grammar subject)
Nouns
Pronouns
Verbs
Adjectives
Sentences
Punctuation

Records
Individual grammar record sheet
Group activity record
Group record sheets (one per grammar subject)
My grammar target record sheets (Two levelled tests)

Teacher resources
Word bank
Speech bubble template
Word web
Word search grid 1 and 2
Mini book and Zig-Zag book templates
Puzzle star template
The word ladder
Word wall blank flash cards
Badges
Book marks
Word wheel - blank
Word wheel cover - one blank / one decorated
Word slides - template
Word slide book
Word searches

Introduction

About the series

Grammar Springboards is a series of three attractive resource books and CD-ROMs designed to make grammar a stimulating and fun learning experience for children of all abilities within KS1 and KS2. Each book is closely linked to the renewed Primary Framework for Literacy and assessment guidelines.

Together the books and the CD-ROMs make an excellent tool for:

- teaching grammar in a range of class settings, as lessons, within groups, individually or as homework.

- teachers and teaching assistants to access easy to use resources and activities for different class situations.

- using elements from the Primary Framework for Literacy units and QCA subject units to bring grammar to life.

- pupil assessment with opportunities for day to day assessment, periodic assessment and transitional assessment with links to Assessment focuses (AFs).

About the book

Each book focuses on the main areas of grammar taught within KS1 and KS2.

These are:

- Nouns

- Pronouns

- Verbs

- Adjectives

- Adverbs

- Sentences

- Punctuation.

Note:' Grammar Springboard Year 1-2' does not have a chapter on adverbs as it is recommended that this area of grammar is introduced in year 3.

At the front of each book there is a Primary Framework for Literacy 'Learning objectives reference chart' which shows what strands and objectives are covered in each grammar lesson and activity.

There are three main sections to the book. They are:

Section 1

Section 1 is set out in chapters covering each of the main grammar areas –nouns, pronouns, verbs, adjectives, adverbs, sentences, punctuation.

Each chapter contains:
Grammar information: Teacher information about the uses and different aspects of the grammar subject including a glossary of terms, examples and word tables.

Ideas Springboard: Fun ideas for wall displays, games and activities for the class, groups or individuals. Some resources for games and activities can be found in 'Teacher Resources' – See 'About the CD-ROM.'

Lesson plans: Suggested lesson plans for the different grammar subjects and objectives.
e.g. Chapter 1 Nouns includes the subjects Common nouns, Proper nouns, Compound nouns etc.

Each lesson has a main teacher led lesson followed by differentiated activities for three ability groups.

Each lesson plan has:
- **Lesson objectives**

- **Resources:** list of suggested resources for the lesson and activities. Resources can be found in 'Lesson resources' on the CD-ROM. See 'About the CD-ROM.'

- **Lesson/activity notes:** Suggestions on setting up resources and suggested grouping and support for the activity groups.

- **Introduction:** Ideas for introducing a grammar subject .

- **Main lesson:**
  Teacher or adult led lesson with class participation.

- **Differentiated group activities:**
  Three bullet point activities.

- **Plenary:**
  Suggestions on ways to reinforce the lesson's objectives.

- **Support:** Ideas for supporting children who may need more reinforcement or consolidation in their learning.

- **Extension:** Ideas and challenges for children who have grasped the main objectives and need to extend their knowledge.

Photocopiable activity worksheets or resources:. Each activity sheet has a definition on the top and simple assessment sentences at the bottom for self assessment and day to day assessment.

Section 2 : Assessment

Periodic Assessment tests: Two levelled short tests to accompany each grammar chapter. The questions cover all the grammar areas taught in each chapter.

Transitional Assessment tests. Two levelled transitional tests that can be used at the end of a school year to judge the progress and understanding of grammar subjects.

Assessment Reference Charts: Writing and reading assessment charts that refers to what levelled assessment focuses (AFs) are covered in each grammar lesson and activity.

Section 3: CD-ROM

The accompanying CD-ROM contains resources which can be used on whiteboards or photocopied.

Lesson resources: Includes resources to accompany each of the lesson plans including texts to highlight or re-model, word and sentence examples, flashcards, information posters, games, templates for word sliders and pictures.

Worksheets: Stand alone photocopiable worksheets for reinforcement, extension, homework and individual assessment. There are two levelled worksheets linked to each grammar subject covered within each chapter, e.g. two worksheets on descriptive adjectives.

Records: These include

- **Individual Grammar Record Sheet:** To be used during an activity for observing or assessing a child's responses and understanding of the objective.

- **Group Activity Record:** To be used for writing observational notes and the children's comments during a group activity.

- **Group Record Charts:** To be used to record when certain children in a specific group have understood different learning objectives.

- **My grammar target record sheet:** A child's own record sheet of achieving the learning objectives of the different grammar subjects. There is one sheet per grammar subject with a tick chart and a design to colour in as they achieve each objective.

Teacher resources: These include:
- Word bank

- Word searches and word search grid templates

- Templates for models and games

- Definitions posters

- Flash cards

- Fun Grammar book marks and badges.

Word Bank: This useful resource can be used by teachers as a quick and easy reference or by children exploring different words and creating their own word banks.

Literacy learning objective reference charts

Strand	Nouns	Pronouns	Verbs	Adjectives	Sentences	Punctuation
Strand 1 Speaking Year 1						
Retell stories, ordering events using story language.					+	+
Tell stories and describe incidents from their own experience in an audible voice.			+		+	
Interpret a text by reading aloud with some variety in pace and emphasis.			+	+	+	
Experiment with and build new stores of words to communicate in different contexts.	+		+	+	+	+
Strand 1 Speaking Year 2						
Speak with clarity and use appropriate intonation when reading and reciting texts.			+		+	
Tell real and imagined stories using the conventions of familiar story language.			+	+	+	
Explain ideas and processes using imaginative and adventurous vocabulary and non-verbal gestures to support communication.	+		+	+	+	+
Strand 2 Listening and responding Year 1						
Listen with sustained concentration, building new stores of words in different contexts.	+	+	+	+	+	+
Listen to and follow instructions accurately, asking for help and clarification if necessary.	+	+	+	+	+	+
Strand 2 Listening and responding Year 2						
Listen to others in class, ask relevant questions and follow instructions.	+	+	+	+	+	+
Listen to talk by an adult, remember some specific points and identify what they have learned.	+	+	+	+	+	+
Strand 3 Group discussion and interaction Year 1						
Take turns to speak, listen to each other's suggestions and talk about what they are going to do.	+	+	+	+	+	+
Ask and answer questions, make relevant contributions, offer suggestions and take turns.	+	+	+	+	+	+
Explain their views to others in a small group, decide how to report the group's views to the class.	+	+	+	+	+	+
Strand 3 Group discussion and interaction Year 2						
Ensure that everyone contributes, allocate tasks, and consider alternatives and reach agreement.	+	+	+	+	+	+
Work effectively in groups by ensuring that each group member takes a turn challenging, supporting and moving on.	+	+	+	+	+	+

Strand	Nouns	Pronouns	Verbs	Adjectives	Sentences	Punctuation
Listen to each other's views and preferences, agree the next steps to take and identify contributions by each group member.	+	+	+	+	+	+
Strand 6 Word structure and spelling Year 1						
Use knowledge of common inflections in spelling, such as plurals, -ly, -er.	+		+			
Strand 6 Word structure and spelling Year 2						
Spell with increasing accuracy and confidence, drawing on word recognition and knowledge of word structure, and spelling patterns including common inflections and use of double letters.	+		+			
Strand 7 Understanding and interpreting texts Year 1						
Identify the main events and characters in stories, and find specific information in simple texts.	+	+	+	+	+	+
Make predictions showing an understanding of ideas, events and characters.				+	+	
Recognise the main elements that shape different texts.		+		+	+	
Explore the effect of patterns of language and repeated words and phrases.	+	+	+	+	+	+
Strand 7 Understanding and interpreting texts Year 2						
Draw together ideas and information from across a whole text, using simple signposts in the text.	+	+	+	+	+	+
Give some reasons why things happen or characters change.				+	+	
Explain organisational features of texts, including alphabetical order, layout, diagrams, captions, hyperlinks and bullet points.					+	+
Use syntax and context to build their store of vocabulary when reading for meaning.						
Explore how particular words are used, including words and expressions with similar meanings.	+	+	+	+	+	+
Strand 8 Engaging and responding to texts Year 1						
Visualise and comment on events, characters and ideas, making imaginative links to their own experiences.				+	+	+
Strand 8 Engaging and responding to texts Year 2						
Explain their reactions to texts, commenting on important aspects.	+	+	+	+	+	+
Strand 9 Creating and shaping texts Year 1						
Independently choose what to write about, plan and follow it through.				+	+	
Use key features of narrative in their own writing.		+		+	+	+
Convey information and ideas in simple non-narrative forms.		+			+	+
Find and use new and interesting words and phrases, including story language.	+	+	+	+	+	+

Strand	Nouns	Pronouns	Verbs	Adjectives	Sentences	Punctuation
Create short simple texts on paper and screen that combine words with images.	+	+	+	+	+	+
Strand 9 Creating and shaping texts Year 2						
Draw on knowledge and experience of texts in deciding and planning what and how to write.	+	+	+	+	+	+
Sustain form in narrative, including use of person and time.		+			+	+
Maintain consistency in non-narrative, including purpose and tense.		+	+		+	+
Make adventurous word and language choices appropriate to the style and purpose of the text.	+	+	+	+	+	+
Strand 10 Text structure and organisation Year 1						
Write chronological and non-chronological texts using simple structures.		+	+	+	+	+
Group written sentences together in chunks of meaning or subject .					+	
Strand 10 Text structure and organisation Year 2						
Use planning to establish clear sections of writing.	+	+	+	+	+	+
Use appropriate language to make sections hang together.					+	
Strand 11 Sentence structure and punctuation Year 1						
Compose and write simple sentences independently to communicate meaning.	x	x	x	x	x	x
Use capital letters and full stops when punctuating simple sentences.	x				x	x
Strand 11 Sentence structure and punctuation Year 2						
Write simple and compound sentences and begin to use subordination in relation to time and reason.					x	
Compose sentences using tense consistently (present and past).			x		x	
Use question marks, and use commas to separate items in a list.					x	x

Chapter 1 – Nouns

Noun Information

Common noun: a word that is used to name people, places, objects or creatures.
e.g. clown, fire-fighter, forest, airport, pen, strawberry, tiger, grasshopper.

Proper noun: a word that gives people, places, objects and events their specific or special names. Proper nouns always begin with a capital letter.
e.g. Mr Benson, Mrs Khan, Doctor Lee, Queen's Avenue, Tesco, Arsenal Football Club, River Thames, Cardiff, Fife, Saturn, Snickers, Monday, April.

Compound noun: a word made up of two nouns.
e.g. snowman, teabag, peanut, sunflower, rainbow, toothbrush, suitcase, footpath.

Singular noun: a noun that names one person, place, object or creature.
e.g. castle, shell, flag, bucket, bird, spade, crab, towel.

Plural noun: a noun that names more than one person, place, object or creature.
Some plural nouns are created by adding -s on the end.
e.g. castles, shells, flags, buckets, birds, spades, crabs, towels.

Some plural nouns are created by adding –es in the end.
e.g. dresses, foxes, princesses, beaches.

Some nouns are both singular and plural.
e.g. sand, sheep, seaweed, deer, trousers, scissors.

Articles

Article: the small words 'the', 'an' and 'a' used before a noun.
They can be a definite or indefinite articles.

'the' is a <u>definite</u> article– it points to a specific thing.
e.g. the egg, the car, the apron, the table, the iceberg, the school.

'an' and 'a' are <u>indefinite</u> articles – they don't point to any specific thing.
e.g. an egg, a car, an apron, a table, an iceberg, a school.

'an' is used before words beginning with a vowel or words with an unsounded 'h'.
e.g. an apple, an elephant, an igloo, an orange, an umbrella, an hotel, an hour.

'an' is <u>not</u> used in front of words beginning with 'u' with a hard sound (ewe),
e.g. a unicorn, a uniform.

'a' is used before words beginning with consonants or words beginning with a hard 'u' (ewe).
e.g. a coat, a slide, a teacher, a monkey, a theatre, a university.

Noun Springboards

Noun ideas

Collect catalogues, brochures and magazines that include examples of the four types of common nouns. Give a group of children one noun category such as 'people' and ask them to cut them out. Let them create labels and display their nouns with the labels as a display.

Let the children research a noun category. For example they can discuss and find out more about peoples jobs and their titles e.g. fire-fighter, doctor, teacher. A class noun list of the workers names can be added onto the board with labels and information about the jobs.

Create graphs from a survey and pictures of the children's favourite nouns of a category e.g. favourite mini-beasts, favourite local places, favourite jobs and favourite food.

Word walls

Create eye catching word walls. One flash card equals one brick. Have several bricks to create the word wall with the children. Have blank cards that the children can write new nouns and add to or make a new word wall shape.
They can be used in a variety of ways.
- Common and proper nouns: - one wall per noun category, e.g. animals, objects, names of countries.

- Making compound nouns.

- Pairs such as single and plural nouns of a noun.

- Word wall for 'an' words and a word wall for 'a' words.

The Word ladder

A similar game to 'Consequences'. In groups of four the children are given strips of paper with four sections (see Word ladder Template – Teacher resources). The children write a noun on the first section, fold over the paper to hide it and pass it to the next child. They then write another noun on the next and so on. After the strip has been completed it is opened up and the children read out the four written nouns.

- **Common nouns:** A child writes an example of a person noun e.g. queen followed by an animal, place and object. They use the four nouns to orally tell a story.

- **Proper nouns:** Choose four categories in advanced and at the end the children use the nouns to tell a story or use the ideas to write a poem.

Word wheel/ Word slide
(see Teacher resources for templates)
The teacher or children add nouns to the wheels or slides to explore and discover other words such as plurals with s, compound nouns. Also a good reinforcement resource.

Pass the book

The children stand in the circle with a child in the middle with his or her eyes closed. The book is passed round the circle until the child in the middle claps. The child then says a letter of the alphabet. The child holding the book has to say four nouns/ proper/plural/ compound nouns (the noun subject is decided before the game starts) before the book is passed around the circle and ends up with them again. If the child does not manage to do it, he/she swaps places with the child in middle.

Matching compound nouns- Fox and geese.

Put the children into a circle. Number the children 1 and 2 alternately around the circle. Give all the 1s a beginning noun of a compound noun on a piece of paper. Give all the 2s the second parts of the compound nouns (the cards should be mixed up). Point to a child who is a number 1 and ask them to shout out their noun. A number 2 that has a noun that makes a compound noun calls out their noun. They jump up and try and chase each other around the circle and then sit down.

Other activity ideas

- I'm thinking of a noun. I'm acting a noun. I'm drawing a noun.

- Hangman.

- Team game when noun cards are put in the right category baskets- speed game.

- Word searches- doing them and creating their own.

- Creating fun nonsense compound nouns with drawings.

- Use pictures and colouring books for the children to find nouns/ more than one thing – plurals and get them to write a list down of what they see.

- Kim's game: - Children look at a picture or a tray of objects before it is taken away. They write a list or say what they can remember.

- Highlighting the proper names used on a simple local map.

- Making a list of local shop names and designing their own shop display boards.

- Make up a product with a special name e.g. Clever Kettle. In small groups, the children have a few minutes to sell it to the rest of the group.

- Fun compound nouns with fonts and colours and texts.

- Happy common noun families/ Happy proper noun families.

- Matching Bingo – e.g. Make a compound noun/ single noun base board and plural noun cards.

- Trump cards/ Fact cards of noun categories.

Common Nouns

Learning Objectives:

• To understand that common nouns name people, creatures, places and objects.

• To identify and use common nouns in sentences.

Resources:

• **Lesson** - 'Noun picture cards' (Lesson resources-CD-ROM). Copy the noun picture card sheets onto thin card and cut them into individual cards.

• **Group 1** – A copy or copies of activity sheet 1, 'Green Street Summer Fair' for each child.

• **Group 2** — Copies of activity sheet 2, 'Lucky Dip Stall' for each child.

• **Group 3** - Copies of activity sheet 3, The Big Noun Wheel' for each child.

Lesson/activity notes

• **Lesson** - Before the lesson, display the noun picture cards around the room.

• **Group 1** – Children work as a discussion group with adult support.

• **Group 2** – Children working individually on activity sheet and then with a partner or group to play a game.

• **Group 3** – Children work individually on activity sheet and as pair-share with their work.

Explain to the children that they are going to do common noun activities set round a summer fair. Put the children into their levelled groups and give out the activities. Spend time moving between the groups to discuss individual children's work and assess their level of understanding.

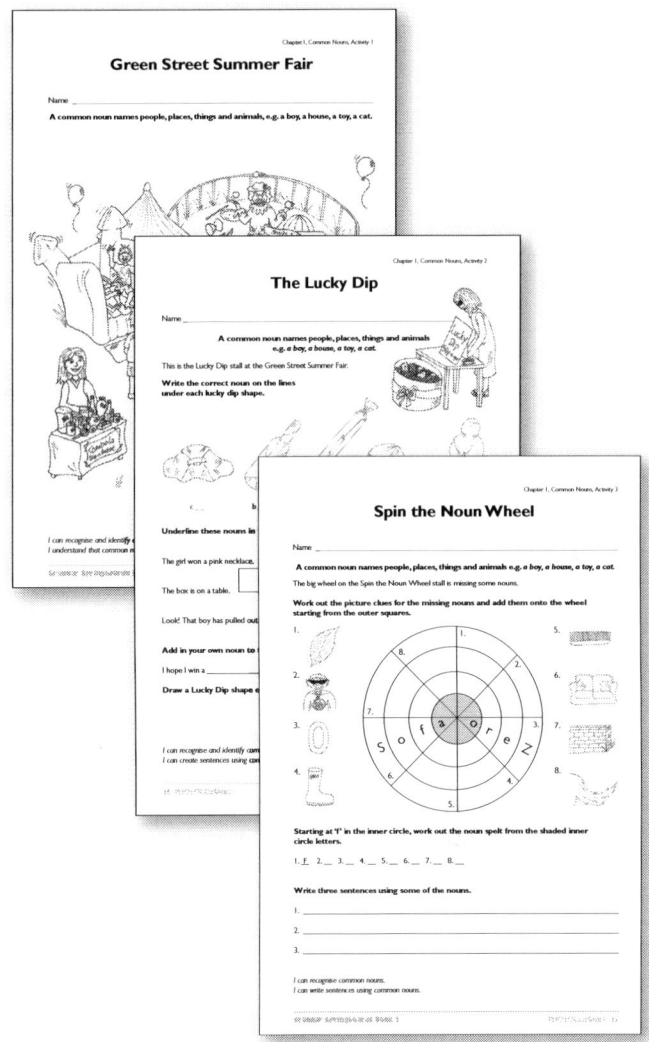

Lesson

Introduction

At the beginning of the lesson, ask the children to look around the room for word and picture cards but not to tell the others what they can see. Explain that they are going to play 'I-Spy' using the cards as subjects. Choose one child to start. When the correct answer is given, ask the child to bring up the card and then attach it to a board in front of the class. Once all the cards have been located and displayed, explain that all the words are common nouns.

Main lesson

Highlight that a common noun's job is to name people, creatures, places and objects. Draw four columns on the white board and at the top of each column write: *'People, Creatures Places, Objects'*. With the children, sort the noun cards into the correct columns. Ask the children for a few more common noun examples and add them to the columns. Using a noun from each group, work with the children to write simple sentences. Do the first one as an example, e.g. 'The <u>boy</u> fell over.' Underline the noun.

Activities

Group 1

• Remind the children what a common noun is and point to a couple of examples e.g. boy, ball.

• Then the children look at the picture 'Green Street Summer Fair' to try and find 20 common nouns.

• This can be done as a discussion group with the children taking turns to find and circle a noun on one copy of the picture or individually with the children finding and circling the nouns on their own copies.

• At the end of the task, look at the chosen nouns. Ask which ones are people nouns, object nouns etc. Record the children's responses as they work.

Group 2:

- Give out the activity sheet 'The Lucky Dip Stall' to each child. If needed, read through the sheet with them.

- Working individually, the children guess the lucky dip presents from their shapes and write the correct noun underneath each present.

- They then underline nouns in a sentence and draw a picture of each one, followed by adding in a noun of their own in a sentence.

- Once the children have completed their worksheets, encourage them to play 'I'm thinking of a noun' with a partner or within their group.

Group 3:

- Give out the activity sheet 'The Big Noun Wheel' to each child within the group.

- Working individually, the children complete the word wheel puzzle by working out the four letter noun words from the picture clues and adding them into the wheel.

- They then create their own sentences using the nouns.

- Encourage the children to share their sentences with each other.

Plenary:

Ten minutes before the end of the lesson, bring the children together. Revise what a common noun does. Ask the class questions such as "What are the four nouns in this sentence? - *The girl went to the tent to have her face painted like a butterfly.*' Finish the lesson by encouraging each child to give you a common noun that names a person, a creature, a place and an object

Support:

Encourage those children who are unconfident in identifying common nouns, to create their own common noun picture book. The children can draw, cut out pictures from magazines, catalogues, take photos etc and add them into their noun books under the four categories.

Extension:

Encourage the children to collect and write down 20 common nouns of people, places, creatures and objects relating to a given subject or topic, e.g. the sea, food. Ask them to draw a picture and write simple captions for each noun.

Green Street Summer Fair

Name _____

A common noun names people, places, things and animals, e.g. a boy, a house, a toy, a cat.

I can recognise and identify common nouns.
I understand that common nouns name people, places, things and animals

The Lucky Dip

Name _____

A common noun names people, places, things and animals
e.g. *a boy, a house, a toy, a cat.*

This is the Lucky Dip stall at the Green Street Summer Fair.

**Write the correct noun on the lines
under each lucky dip shape.**

c _ _   b _ _   p _ _   b _ _ _   d _ _ _

Underline these nouns in the sentences. Draw a picture for each noun in the boxes.

The girl won a pink necklace.

The box is on a table.

Look! That boy has pulled out a yoyo!

Add in your own noun to this sentence.

I hope I win a _____ from the Lucky Dip box.

Draw a Lucky Dip shape of a noun below. Can a friend guess what it is?

I can recognise and identify common nouns.
I can create sentences using common nouns.

Spin the Noun Wheel

Name _____

A common noun names people, places, things and animals e.g. *a boy, a house, a toy, a cat.*

The big wheel on the Spin the Noun Wheel stall is missing some nouns.

Work out the picture clues for the missing nouns and add them onto the wheel starting from the outer squares.

1.

2.

3.

4.

5.

6.

7.

8.

Starting at 'f' in the inner circle, work out the noun spelt from the shaded inner circle letters.

1. F   2. __   3. __   4. __   5. __   6. __   7. __   8. __

Write three sentences using some of the nouns.

1. _____

2. _____

3. _____

I can recognise common nouns.
I can write sentences using common nouns.

Proper Nouns

Learning Objectives:

- To understand that proper nouns give people, places, objects and events their given or special names.

- To learn that proper nouns always begin with a capital letter.

- To understand the difference between a proper noun and a common noun.

Resources:

- **Lesson** - Proper noun category headings such as favourite film, favourite day of the week, favourite football club, favourite country, favourite name written on separate pieces of paper. Put one on each table.

- **Group 1** - Copy and cut up the cards from activity sheet 1 'Proper nouns or common nouns?' Two tins with 'Proper Nouns' labelled in one and 'Common Nouns' labelled on the other.

- **Group 2** - Copies of activity sheet 2 'Down at the Shops' for each child.

- **Group 3** – Copies of activity sheet 3 'Juppton' for each child. A local map.

Lesson/activity notes:

- **Lesson** - This lesson can be adapted from a class to a group exercise by giving each child a heading. Before the lesson put the proper noun headings on each table. Spread the children around the tables in the class.

- **Group 1** – Working as a discussion group with adult support.

- **Group 2** –Working individually on activity sheet and then as a discussion group.

- **Group 3** - Working individually on activity sheet and then as a group to look at a local map.

Lesson

Introduction

At the beginning of the lesson, briefly revise examples of common nouns. Explain to the class that they going to learn about another type of noun called a proper noun. Ask each table of children to look at the favourite proper noun subject on the paper and to individually think of their favourite example e.g. favourite country-India. Encourage them to briefly discuss why to the others in their group.

Main lesson

Write the headings on the board and ask each group to tell the class of their choices. Record them under each relevant heading. Once all the groups have given their answers, read through the words under each heading. Explain to the children that all the names are proper nouns. They are the special or given names of people, places, events, and clubs and always start with a capital letter.

Explain that they are going to investigate proper nouns using different activities set round a fictional town. Put the children into their levelled groups. Spend time moving between the groups to discuss individual children's work and assess their level of understanding.

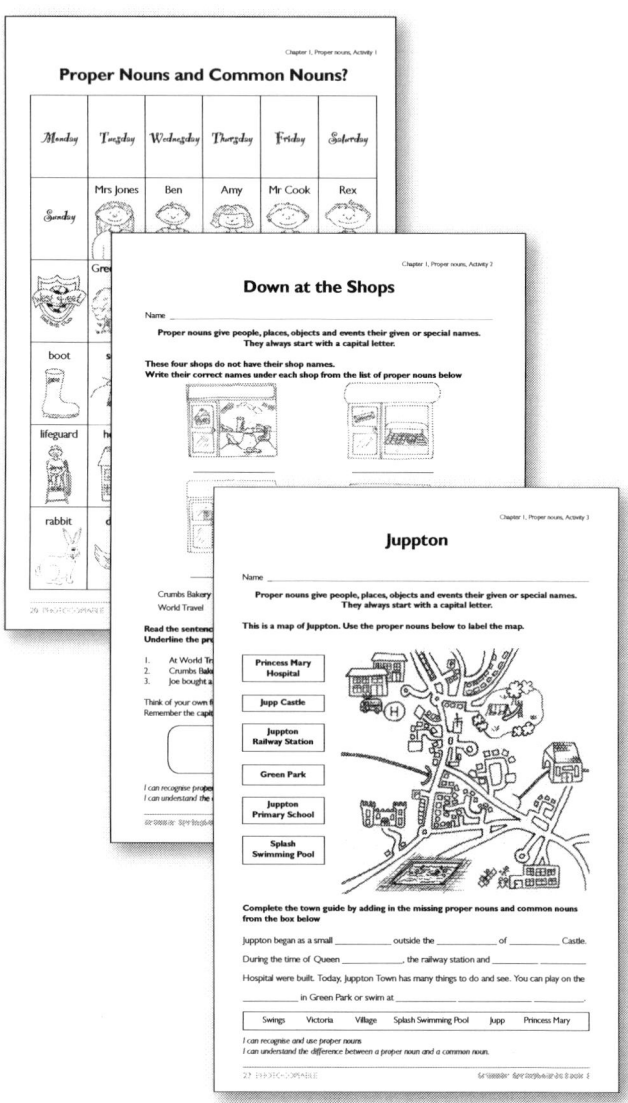

Activities

Group 1

- Put the 'Proper Nouns' and 'Common Nouns' tins and the shuffled pile of 'Proper nouns or common nouns?' cards in front of the children.

- Taking turns, let a child pick up a card and read it out. Ask *'Should it go in the proper nouns tin or the common nouns tin?'*

- As they make their choice, ask the children their reasons. Record their responses.

- Once the cards are gone, empty the tins and spread out the cards.

- Discuss why the cards in the 'Proper Noun' tin are proper nouns. Highlight the capital letters.

- Ask the children for proper noun examples in their local area e.g. shop names, street names.

Group 2

- Give out copies of the activity 2 sheet, 'Down at the Shops', to each child.

- Working individually, the children find the correct proper noun names of four shops from a list of proper nouns and write them under each shop.

- They then read three sentences and underline the proper nouns in red and underline the common nouns in blue.

- Finally they create their own shop name and draw its shop sign.

- Encourage the children to discuss in pairs or as a small group, proper noun shop names in their local area. Which ones stand out? Why? Do they all start with capital letters?

Group 3

- Give out copies of Activity 3 sheet 'Juppton' to each child.

- Working individually, the children have to match and label proper noun names to places on a drawn town map.
- They then have to add in the missing proper nouns and common nouns in a town guide text.

- If time, show the children a map of their local area and encourage them as group to find proper nouns.

Plenary

Before the end of the lesson, bring all the groups together. Revise proper nouns by asking them for the proper noun of a month, a weekday, a car, a name, a football club, a country, a special event, a restaurant etc. Write the answers on the board and ask the children why they are proper nouns and what should they always begin with.

Support:

Encourage the children to collect proper noun examples from different groups to create a display, e.g. copy out car names such as Honda, Ford from magazines and match them to photos, cut out cereal packet names, collect chocolate bar wrappers. Label each group with the common noun e.g. cars, cereals and each item with their proper noun name.

Extension:

Ask the children to make proper noun class surveys of different subjects, e.g. favourite month, favourite films, favourite chocolate. Suggest that they offer a set choice of proper noun names e.g. favourite author out of choice of five. How would they show their results? E.g. graphs.

Proper Nouns and Common Nouns?

Monday	Tuesday	Wednesday	Thursday	Friday	Saturday
Sunday	Mrs Jones	Ben	Amy	Mr Cook	Rex
West Street Football Club	Green Park	Splash Pool	Hop Street	Vera's Vets	Yum Food Shop
boot	scarf	slide	swing	football	swimmer
lifeguard	house	car	tree	bicycle	cat
rabbit	duck	apple	carrot	bread	milk

Down at the Shops

Name _____

Proper nouns give people, places, objects and events their given or special names.
They always start with a capital letter.

These four shops do not have their shop names.
Write their correct names under each shop from the list of proper nouns below

_____

_____

_____

_____

Crumbs Bakery	River Trent	Everest	France	Teddies and Toys
World Travel	London	Emily	Tightfit Shoes	Rose Street

Read the sentences below.
Underline the proper nouns in red and the common nouns in blue.

1.   At World Travel, Jem decided he wanted to go to India for his holiday.
2.   Crumbs Bakery sell chocolate doughnuts only on Monday and Friday.
3.   Joe bought a Zoomer Robot as a present for his best friend, Jordan.

Think of your own fun shop name. Write and draw your fun shop sign in the space below.
Remember the capital letters.

I can recognise proper noun
I can understand the difference between a proper noun and a common noun.

Juppton

Name _____

**Proper nouns give people, places, objects and events their given or special names.
They always start with a capital letter.**

This is a map of Juppton. Use the proper nouns below to label the map.

| Princess Mary Hospital |

| Jupp Castle |

| Juppton Railway Station |

| Green Park |

| Juppton Primary School |

| Splash Swimming Pool |

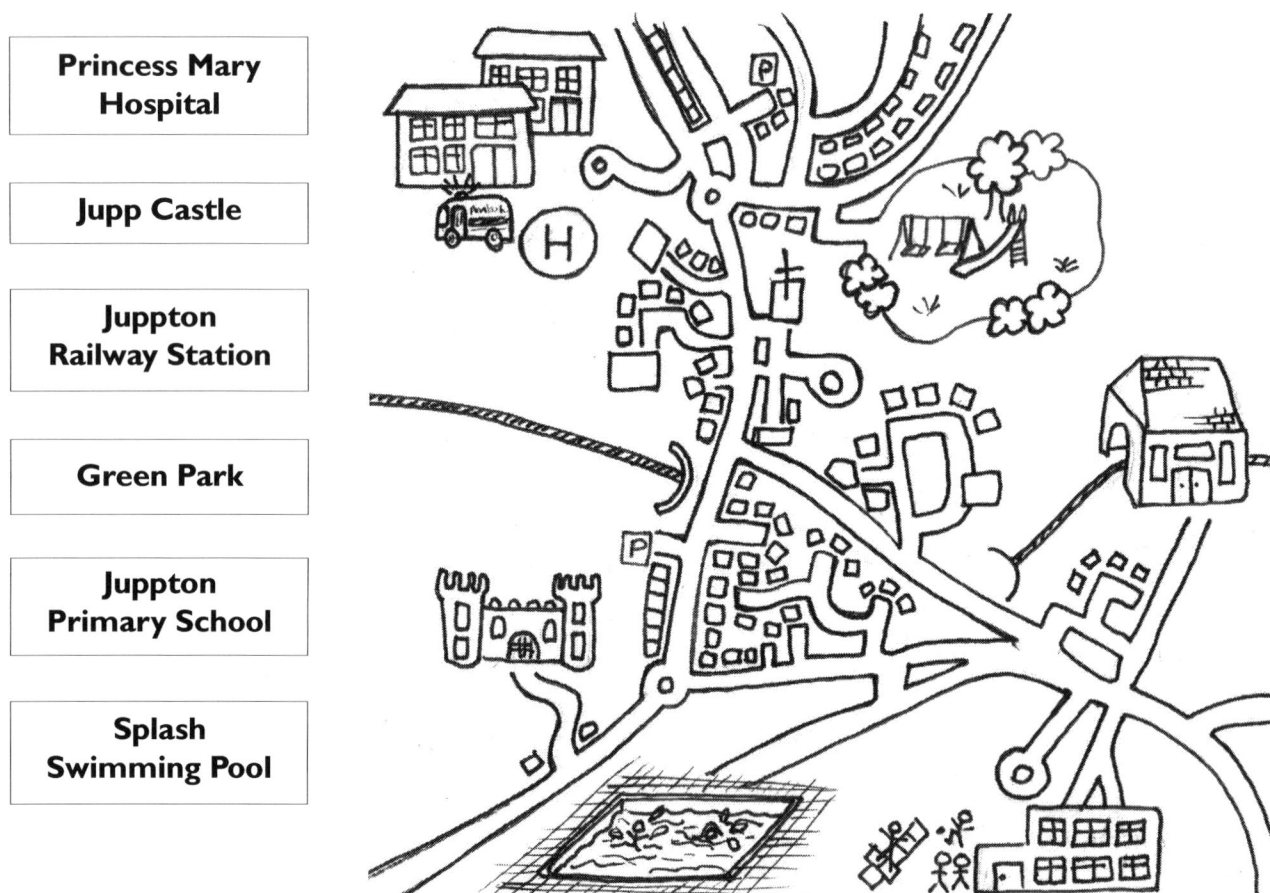

Complete the town guide by adding in the missing proper nouns and common nouns from the box below

Juppton began as a small _____ outside the _____ of _____ Castle.

During the time of Queen _____, the railway station and _____ _____

Hospital were built. Today, Juppton Town has many things to do and see. You can play on the

_____ in Green Park or swim at _____ _____ _____.

| Swings | Victoria | Village | Splash Swimming Pool | Jupp | Princess Mary |

I can recognise and use proper nouns
I can understand the difference between a proper noun and a common noun.

Compound nouns

Learning Objectives:

- To understand that a compound noun is made of two nouns

- To identify and use compound nouns.

Resources:

- **Lesson** - 'Compound noun cards 1 and 2' (Lesson resources CD-ROM). Copy and cut up the sheets into individual cards.

- **Group 1** - 'Professor Compound's noun word machine' (Lesson resources instructions on CD-ROM) , 'Compound noun picture cards-1', Activity sheet 1.2 'Compound noun picture cards 2'. Activity sheets per pair or group. Activity sheet 1.

- **Group 2** – 'Compound noun maker' and 'Compound noun slide strips', for each pair of children and copies onto card of 'Word slide strips' (Lesson resources -CD-ROM). Paper and pencils, Copy and cut out the compound noun maker/strips.

- **Group 3** – 'Professor Compound's card game' (Lesson resources CD-ROM.) Make up the cards before the lesson.

Lesson/activity notes

- **Lesson** - Before the lesson, set out the 'Compound noun cards 2' on tables around the classroom. Keep the 'Compound noun cards 1' with you. If possible start the lesson away from the class tables.

- **Group 1** – Children work as a small discussion group with adult support.

- **Group 2** – Children working in pairs and then share with another pair. Need adult/teacher support.

- **Group 3** – Children work as one group or groups of three or more to playa card game.

Lesson

Introduction

Draw a large door on the white board and write 'door' in the middle. Explain to the children that they are going to help you think of words that start with the word 'door'. Start off with write 'doorstep'. Highlight how the word is made from the two nouns, 'door' and 'step'. Explain that words made up from two words are called compound nouns. 'Encourage the children to think of a few more compound nouns beginning with 'door' and write them by the door shape, e.g. doorknob, doorbell, doorman.

Main lesson

Put the children into mixed pairs. Give each pair a card from 'Compound noun cards 1'. Explain that they need to search the tables for a second noun card to make a compound noun. Show two cards as an example e.g. 'hair' 'brush'. Once they have made their compound noun, they must think of a sentence they can use it in. Ask each pair of children to show and read out their compound noun and say their sentence.

Explain to the children that they are going to work on compound noun activities. Put the children into their levelled groups and give out the activities. Spend time moving between the groups to discuss individual children's work and assess their level of understanding.

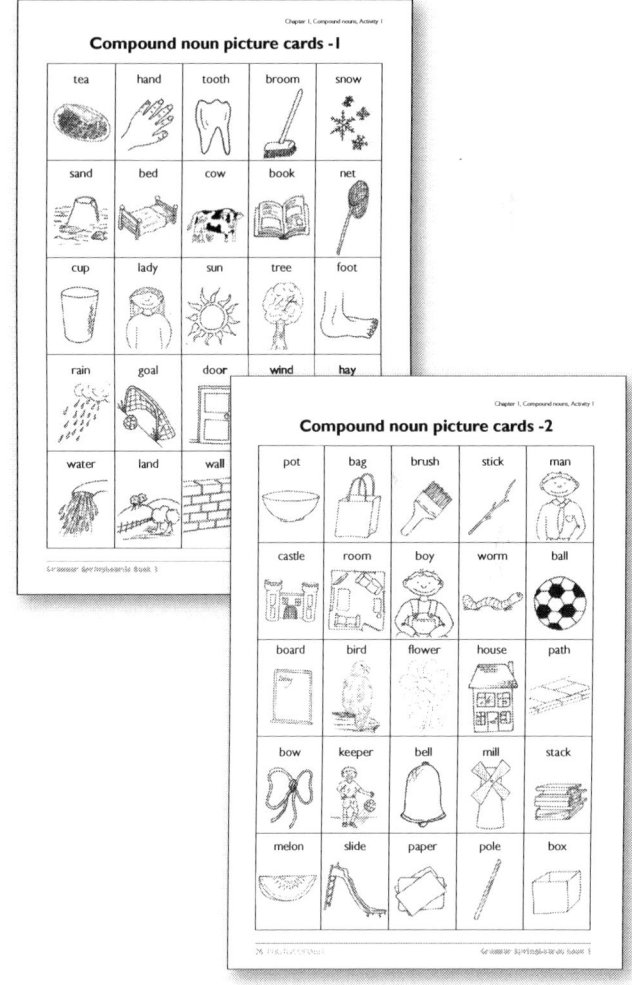

Activities

Group 1

- Put 'Professor Compound's noun machine' in front of the children with the first set of picture compound noun cards in a pile and the second set laid out picture up on the table.

- Ask a child to feed a card from pile one through the machine. Ask the child what the picture noun is.

- Ask them to find a picture noun from the laid out cards that could be added at the end of the first picture noun to make a compound noun, e.g. teapot.

- Write out the compound noun out on paper and put it by the two cards.

- Let the children take turns until all the compound nouns are found. Can they make any more compound nouns from the cards, e.g. teabag?

Group 2

- Give out the 'Compound noun maker,' several 'Compound noun slide strips' and a blank piece of paper to each pair of children.

- Ask the children to make a list of eight compound nouns.

- When they have made their list, ask them to write the first nouns on one word slide strip and the second nouns on the other.

- Let them attach the two strips into their 'Compound noun maker' and then swap it with another pair.

- Ask the children to use the swapped 'Compound noun maker' to find compound nouns and write simple sentences with them.

Group 3

- Shuffle the set of 'Professor Compound's card game' cards and deal them all out to the children.

- The children look at their cards for compound word matches and then place them face up on the table.

- One child starts by choosing a card from the child to their left. If it matches one of their cards they put the pair down if not it stays in their hand.

- The game continues with the next child picking a card from the left.

- The game ends when one child is left with the 'Professor Compound card'.

- Ask the children in turn what their compound nouns mean and to make sentences using them.

Plenary

Before the end of the lesson, bring all the groups together. The children together and ask the children for different examples of a compound noun. Ask what a compound noun is made of two nouns. If time, have fun and create nonsense compound nouns e.g. socksausage.

Support

Encourage the children to create and draw three of their own compound noun picture cards for 'Professor Compound's word machine' game. They can see if another child or children can make the compound nouns and vice versa.

Extension

Highlight that some words such as 'moonlight' or 'handstand 'are made up of a noun and verb. These are called compound words. Encourage the children to make small books of compound nouns and compound words with comic style illustrations and the nouns and verbs written underneath.

Compound noun picture cards -1

tea	hand	tooth	broom	snow
sand	bed	cow	book	net
cup	lady	sun	tree	foot
rain	goal	door	wind	hay
water	land	wall	flag	letter

Compound noun picture cards -2

pot	bag	brush	stick	man
castle	room	boy	worm	ball
board	bird	flower	house	path
bow	keeper	bell	mill	stack
melon	slide	paper	pole	box

Plural nouns ending in 's'

Learning Objectives:
- To understand that nouns that name more than one thing are called plurals.

- To recognise how some nouns can become plurals by adding -s on the end.

Resources:
- **Lesson** - Two shells, 'A seaside letter' (lesson resources-CD ROM). Board.

- **Group 1**- Copies of activity sheet 1 'At the Seaside' for each child.

- **Group 2** – Copies of activity sheet 2 'Beachcombing' for each child. Paper and pencils.

- **Group 3 -** Copies of activity sheet 3 'Seaside postcards', for each child. Access to books.

Lesson/activity notes:
- **Lesson** – Have a whiteboard to show 'A seaside letter' from CD-ROM or show a copy that is large enough for all the children to see.

- **Group 1** – Children work individually on the activity sheet with adult support.

- **Group 2** – Children work individually on their activity sheets. Work in a small group or pairs to list more plural seaside nouns.

- **Group 3** – Children work individually on their activity sheet. They pair share their work.

Lesson

Introduction
Hold up one shell. Say to the children, *'I have bought something from the seaside. What is it?'* The children should answer, *"A shell."* Write the word on the whiteboard. Hold up two shells and ask them what you gave got. They should say *'shells.'* Write the word 'shells' on the board. Ask the children what letter at the end of 'shells' shows that there is more than one. They should answer 's'. Explain that a noun that names more than one thing is called a plural. Write 'plural' above the word 'shells'.

Main
Explain to the children that you are going to read a letter written about a day at the seaside. Ask the children to listen carefully for plural nouns. When they hear a plural, ask them to put their hand up. Read 'A seaside letter' slowly and take note which children put their hands up when they hear a plural noun. When you have finished, ask the children to tell you which plural nouns they heard whilst you write them in a column on the board.

With the children's help write the singular nouns next to the plurals. Ask the children *'How do these single nouns become plural nouns?'* They should say. *'By adding 's' at the ends.'*

Explain that they are going to investigate plural nouns that end in –s using different activities set at the seaside. Put the children into their levelled groups. Spend time moving between the groups to discuss individual children's work and assess their level of understanding.

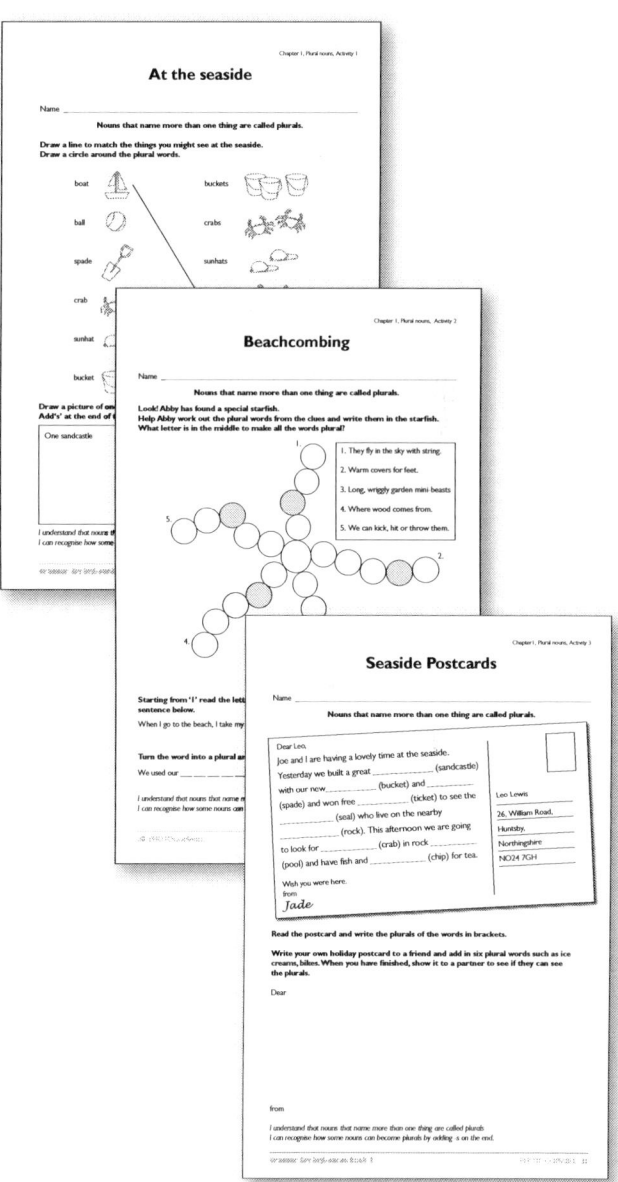

Activities

Group 1
- Give out the copies of activity sheet 1 'At the Seaside' to each of the children.

- The adult support or teacher reads the instructions with the children.

- Working individually, the children match the singular nouns with their plural forms by drawing lines to connect the two.

- They then put a circle around the plural nouns. Ask the children to point to the s at the end of the plural nouns.

- The children then draw a picture of one sandcastle and a picture of two sandcastles.

- At the end of the activity, take note whether the children independently add s to 'sandcastle' to make it a plural noun.

Group 2

- Give out the copies of the activity sheet 2 'Beachcombing' to the children.

- Working individually, the children solve a word puzzle with plural answers.

- Ask the children what letter at the end of the all nouns makes them plurals.

- Within the solved puzzle they will find a word that they use in sentences in both singular and plural forms.

- If time, ask the children to work together in pairs to list more seaside plural nouns ending with 's'.

Group 3

- Give out the copies of activity sheet 3 'Seaside Postcards' to the children.

- Working individually, the children add in the correct plural nouns within a postcard text.

- They then write their own holiday postcard with four plurals within the text. Give out spare paper for the children to workout their text if needed.

- Encourage them to share their text with a partner. Can they see the plurals in the text? What other ones could they add?

Plenary

Before the end of the lesson, bring all the groups together. Draw a face on the board and write the word 'face' above it. Ask the children *'What is a noun that names more than one thing or person?'* They should say *'plural'*. Draw another face next to the other one and ask *'What letter do I add to turn 'face' into 'faces? 'They should say's'*. Draw a big smile on the faces.

Support

To reinforce the idea of plural nouns ending with 's', play simple games using plural and single noun flash cards. For example, shuffle out singular and plural noun cards together and lay them out for the children to put into pairs.

Extension

Highlight that some single nouns can also be plurals, such as 'sand', 'fish', 'gold', and 'sheep'. Ask the children to research similar noun plurals e.g. deer, pants, trousers, seaweed. Put a list up on a display area or create a poster for the children to add to when they come across these plural nouns.

At the seaside

Name _____

Nouns that name more than one thing are called plurals.

Draw a line to match the things you might see at the seaside.
Draw a circle around the plural words.

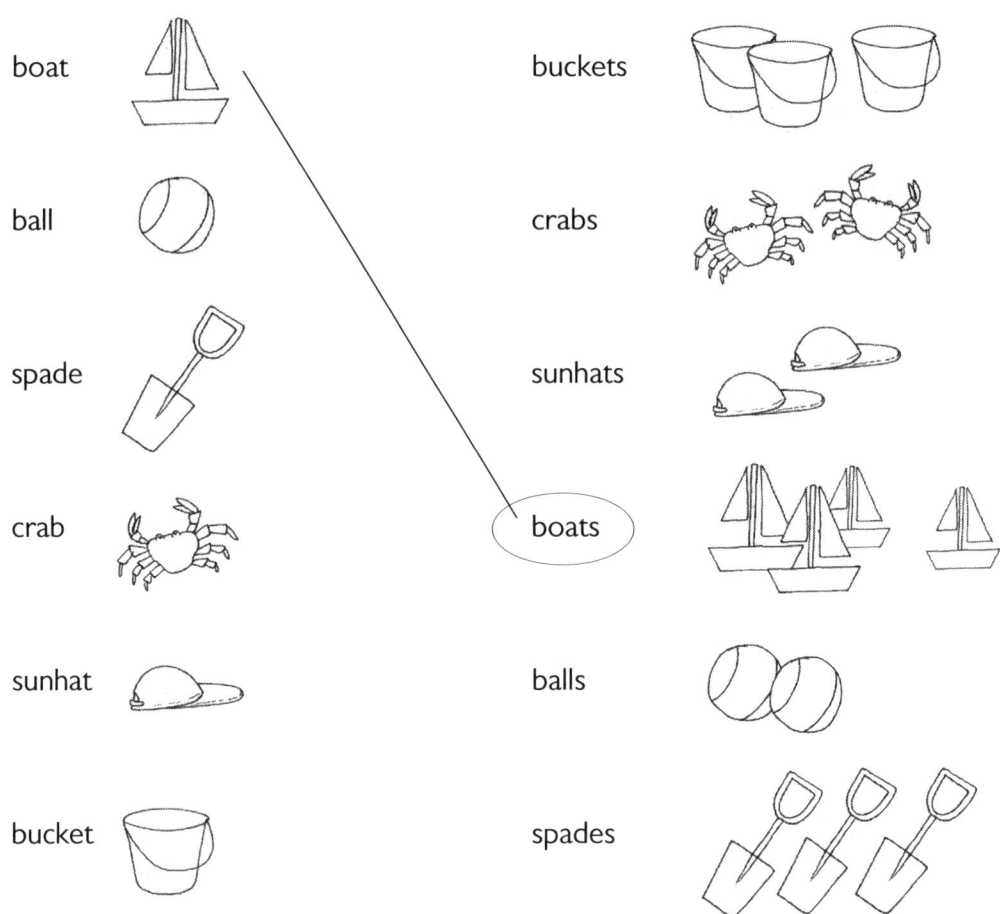

boat

ball

spade

crab

sunhat

bucket

buckets

crabs

sunhats

boats

balls

spades

Draw a picture of one sandcastle in the first box and two sandcastles in the second box.
Add 's' at the end of the word to make it a plural.

One sandcastle	Two sandcastle _

I understand that nouns that name more than one thing are called plurals
I can recognise how some nouns can become plurals by adding -s on the end.

Beachcombing

Name _____

Nouns that name more than one thing are called plurals.

Look! Abby has found a special starfish.
Help Abby work out the plural words from the clues and write them in the starfish.
What letter is in the middle to make all the words plural?

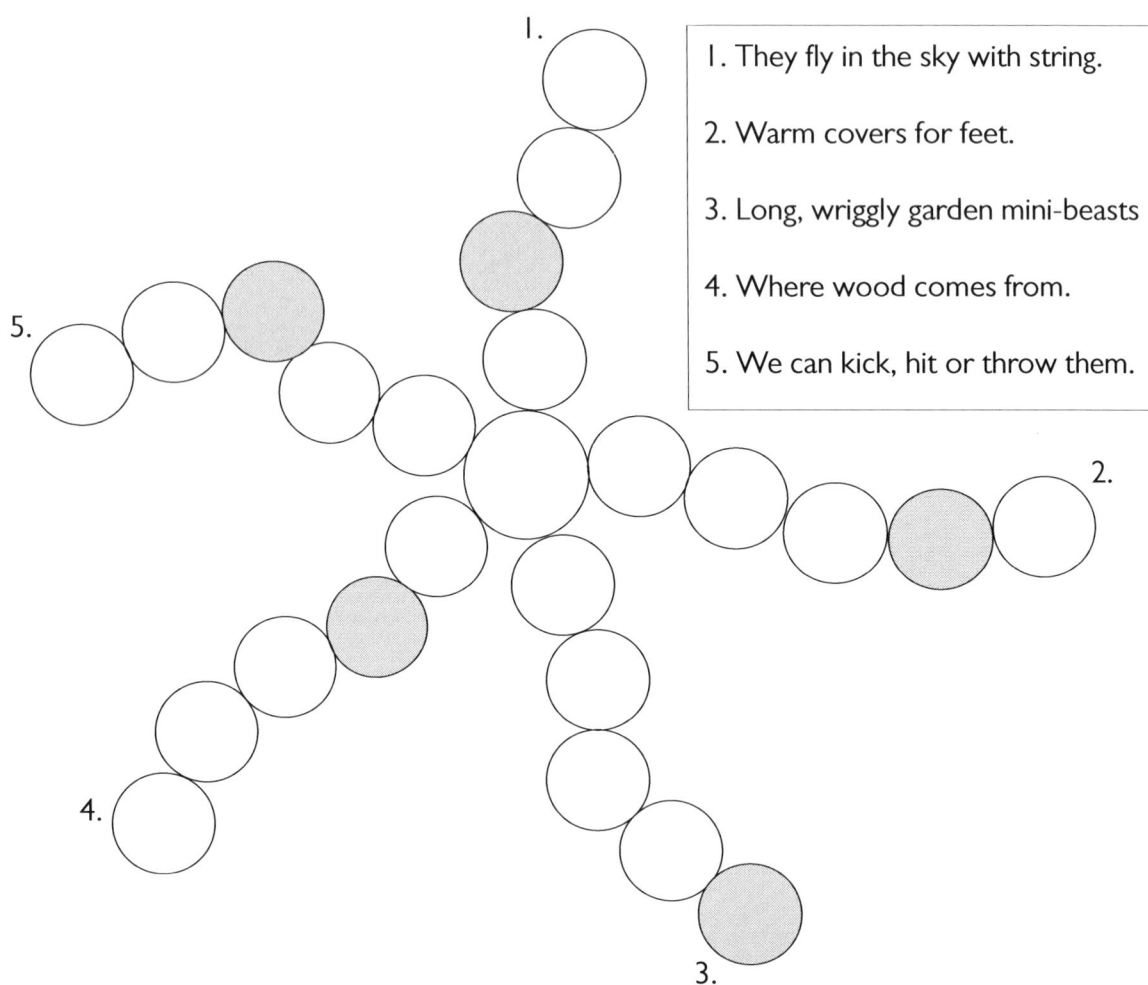

1. They fly in the sky with string.

2. Warm covers for feet.

3. Long, wriggly garden mini-beasts

4. Where wood comes from.

5. We can kick, hit or throw them.

Starting from '1' read the letters in the dark circles to find the word that completes the sentence below.

When I go to the beach, I take my ___ ___ ___ ___ ___.

Turn the word into a plural and complete this sentence.

We used our ___ ___ ___ ___ ___ ___ after we had a swim in the sea.

I understand that nouns that name more than one thing are called plurals
I can recognise how some nouns can become plurals by adding -s on the end.

Seaside Postcards

Name _____

Nouns that name more than one thing are called plurals.

Dear Leo,

Joe and I are having a lovely time at the seaside. Yesterday we built a great _____ (sandcastle) with our new _____ (bucket) and _____ (spade) and won free _____ (ticket) to see the _____ (seal) who live on the nearby _____ (rock). This afternoon we are going to look for _____ (crab) in rock _____ (pool) and have fish and _____ (chip) for tea.

Wish you were here.
from
Jade

Leo Lewis

26, William Road,

Huntsby,

Northingshire

NO24 7GH

Read the postcard and write the plurals of the words in brackets.

Write your own holiday postcard to a friend and add in six plural words such as ice creams, bikes. When you have finished, show it to a partner to see if they can see the plurals.

Dear

from

I understand that nouns that name more than one thing are called plurals
I can recognise how some nouns can become plurals by adding -s on the end.

Articles 'an' and 'a'

Learning Objectives:

- To understand that the word 'an' goes in front of words beginning with vowels.

- To understand that the word 'a' goes in front of words beginning with consonants.

- To identify and use 'a' and 'an'.

Resources:

- **Lesson** - 'an' and 'a' cards – (lesson resources-CD ROM) Copy and cut out the 'an and 'a' to hold up to the class.

- **Group 1** - Scissors, glue, pictures of nouns from catalogues, magazines etc. Two A4 pieces of sugar paper per child.

- **Group 2** –copies of activity 1 'A line poem' for each child.

- **Group 3** – copies of activity 2- 'Riddle poems' for each child, dictionaries/wordbank.

Lesson/activity notes:

- **Lesson:** Note: All words beginning with U and sound like 'ewe', have 'a' in front not 'an'. e.g. a unicorn, a uniform etc

- **Group 1** - Children work individually with adult support.

- **Group 2**- Children work individually on the activity and share their work with a partner or the group.

- **Group 3** – Children work individually on the activity. They can work on their own or with a partner to create a riddle poem.

Lesson

Introduction

With the children, briefly revise consonants and vowels letters. Write the five vowels on the board. Explain that you would like to introduce a little word that goes in front of nouns beginning with a vowel. Hold up the 'an' card and ask the children to say it with you.

Main lesson

Ask the children for an example of a noun beginning with each of the vowels and write them on a board e.g. axe, egg, igloo, orange, umbrella. Write 'an' in front of the first vowel noun and ask the children to read it out loud, e.g. an apple. Do the same with all the other vowels. Highlight the rule for 'u' words. Show the children the 'a' card. Explain that it goes in front of words beginning with consonants. Write a few examples on the board.

Working in pairs, ask the children to mime a noun beginning with a vowel and a noun beginning with a consonant for the rest of the class. Highlight to the rest of the class that they must use 'an' or 'a' with their answers. Once the nouns have been guessed, write them on the board with the 'an' nouns in one column and the 'a' nouns in another.

Explain that they are going to investigate 'an' and 'a' using different activities. Put the children into their levelled groups. Spend time moving between the groups to discuss individual children's work and assess their level of understanding.

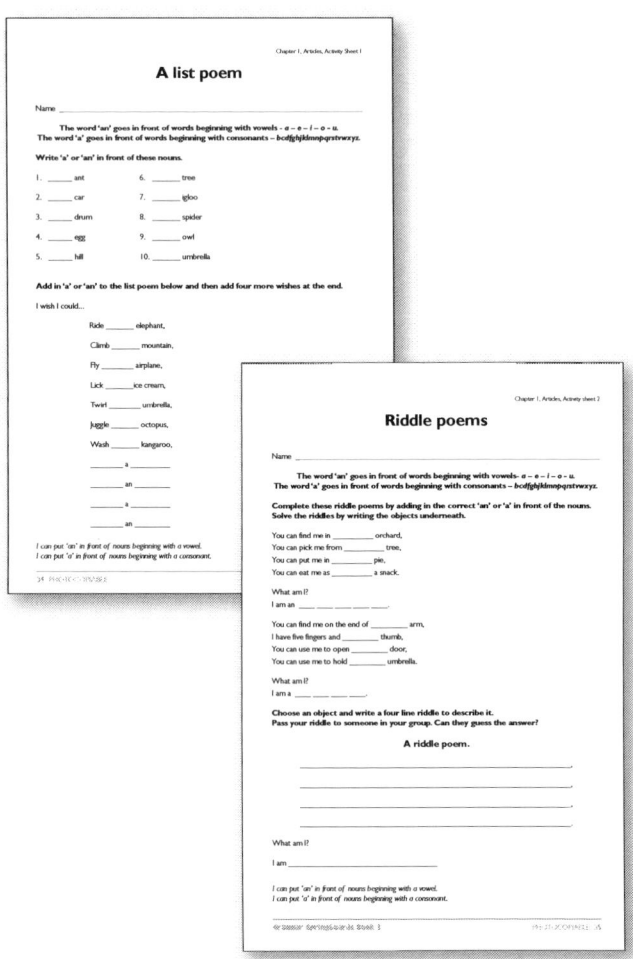

Activities

Group 1

- Explain to the children that they are going to make two posters to show 'an' nouns and 'a' words.

- Give the children the two A4 pieces of paper- one for 'an' nouns and the other for 'a' nouns and a range of catalogues, pictures and magazines.

- Ask the children to cut out six nouns that begin with vowels and six nouns that begin with consonants.

- As the children stick their pictures on their posters, ask them to say the nouns using the 'an' or 'a' word first.

- Write the nouns for the children to copy under the pictures. Ask them to write 'an' or 'a' before each word and underline the first letter of the nouns.

- Let the children share their work and display the posters in the classroom.

Group 2

- Give out the copies of the activity sheet 1 'A list poem' to the children.

- Working individually, they add 'an' or 'a' to the beginning of a list of nouns.

- They then are asked to fill in the list poem using 'a' and 'an'.

- The children complete the poem by writing the last two lines in their own words using 'an' and 'a' before a vowel word and a consonant word.

- Encourage the children to share their poem endings within their group.

Group 3

- Give out the copies of the activity sheet 2 'Riddle poems' and dictionaries or the word bank for 'an' words to the children.

- The children complete the riddles by filling in the 'an' and 'a' by the correct nouns and solving the riddles.

- The children can then work individually or with a partner to create a riddle within a writing frame using a mix of nouns beginning with vowels and consonants preceded by 'an' or 'a'.

Plenary

Before the end of the lesson, bring all the groups together. Ask each group for examples of their work. Praise and highlight good examples. Hold up 'an' card. Ask the children when it should be used. The children should say *'in front of words beginning with vowels.'* Hold up the 'a' card and ask the children when it should be used. They should reply, *'in front of words beginning with consonants.'*

Support

When working on spelling or reading of words beginning with vowels and consonants, encourage the children to say 'an or 'a' before each one.

Extension

Highlight that words with silent 'h' such as 'hotel' also start with 'an'. Encourage the children to sound out the phonic sound and then ask them to see if they can find a few more words that have a silent 'h'.

A list poem

Name _____

The word 'an' goes in front of words beginning with vowels - _a – e – i – o - u._
The word 'a' goes in front of words beginning with consonants – _bcdfghjklmnpqrstvwxyz._

Write 'a' or 'an' in front of these nouns.

1. _____ ant

2. _____ car

3. _____ drum

4. _____ egg

5. _____ hill

6. _____ tree

7. _____ igloo

8. _____ spider

9. _____ owl

10. _____ umbrella

Add in 'a' or 'an' to the list poem below and then add four more wishes at the end.

I wish I could...

Ride _____ elephant,

Climb _____ mountain,

Fly _____ airplane,

Lick _____ ice cream,

Twirl _____ umbrella,

Juggle _____ octopus,

Wash _____ kangaroo,

_____ a _____

_____ an _____

_____ a _____

_____ an _____

I can put 'an' in front of nouns beginning with a vowel.
I can put 'a' in front of nouns beginning with a consonant.

Riddle poems

Name _____

The word 'an' goes in front of words beginning with vowels- *a – e – i – o - u*.
The word 'a' goes in front of words beginning with consonants – *bcdfghjklmnpqrstvwxyz*.

Complete these riddle poems by adding in the correct 'an' or 'a' in front of the nouns.
Solve the riddles by writing the objects underneath.

You can find me in _____ orchard,

You can pick me from _____ tree,

You can put me in _____ pie,

You can eat me as _____ a snack.

What am I?

I am an ____ ____ ____ ____ ____.

You can find me on the end of _____ arm,

I have five fingers and _____ thumb,

You can use me to open _____ door,

You can use me to hold _____ umbrella.

What am I?

I am a ____ ____ ____ ____.

Choose an object and write a four line riddle to describe it.
Pass your riddle to someone in your group. Can they guess the answer?

A riddle poem.

_____,

_____,

_____,

_____.

What am I?

I am _____

I can put 'an' in front of nouns beginning with a vowel.
I can put 'a' in front of nouns beginning with a consonant.

Chapter 2 – Pronouns

Pronoun Information

Pronoun: a word that can replace a noun or noun phrase to make a text flow and cut down on repetition.

e.g. *Ali ran to the park. Ali went on the swings.*' becomes '*Ali ran to the park. He went on the swings.*'

Types of pronouns

Personal pronouns: words that replace names of people, places, objects and creatures.

- Subject personal pronouns: I, you, she, he, we, it and they. These pronouns replace the names of people or objects that do actions.
  e.g. '*Josh kicked the ball.*' becomes '*He liked the ball*'.

- Object personal pronouns: me, you, her, him, it, us and them. These pronouns replace the names of the people or things that are affected by an action.
  e.g. '*Kim hugged Gran.*' becomes '*Kim hugged her.*'

Singular pronouns: words that replace single nouns such as one person or one object.
I, my, me, mine, you, your, yours, she, her, hers, he, him, his, it, its.
e.g. '*Mrs King read Harry's letter.*' becomes '*She read his letter.*'
'*The snake hissed. The snake was cross.*' becomes '*The snake hissed. It was cross.*'

Plural pronouns: words that replace plural nouns such as more than one person or object.
we, us, our, ours, you, your, yours, they, them, their, theirs.
e.g. '*Tim let the fish go.*' becomes '*Tim let them go.*'

Other pronouns.

Interrogative pronouns: question words that replace a person or objects that is being asked about.
Who? Whose? Which? What? Whom?
e.g. *Who is the boss? What is his address? Whose shoes are these?*

Demonstrative pronouns: words that replace singular or plural nouns and highlight the location of an object. – this, that, these, those.
e.g. '*You get these crisps and I'll get the crisps over there.*' becomes '*You get these crisps and I'll get those.*'

Possessive pronouns: words that are used to replace a noun to show ownership.
mine, his, hers, its, yours, ours, theirs.
e.g. '*This is Sara's book and this is your book.*' becomes '*This is Sara's book and this is yours.*'

Pronoun Springboards

Pronoun word wall

Create a pronoun word wall. Walls could include a singular pronoun wall, plural pronoun wall and simple sentences wall with the pronoun cards in a different colour.

Pronoun sentence display.

Have pronoun flash cards on a display board with other words so that the children could use them to make up simple sentences when they are asked or voluntarily in a quiet time.

The missing pronouns

Have a pronoun challenge. Have a sentence on the display board and say that someone has taken the pronouns out. Ask the children if they could add them back in. Change the sentences over the week and get the children watch out and add in the missing pronouns.

Pronoun songs and rhymes

Let the children listen to or read a poem a nursery rhyme or a simple song, e.g. 'Sing a song of sixpence'. .Ask the children to make a mark on a piece of paper for every time they hear a pronoun. You could also do this with short stories.

A pronoun rug

Draw a big patchwork rug on paper. Put a variety of pronouns in each shape and then fill the rest of the shapes with nouns, verbs, adjectives etc. Ask the children to colour in all the pronouns in one colour and the other words in another colour. For more able children you could ask them to colour in nouns in one colour and verbs in another etc.

Adding pronouns

1. Copy a simple text from a picture book or short story onto the computer and ask the children to delete the personal nouns such as names and type in personal nouns. Discuss the difference.

2. Make copies of a story text or poem relating to the child's ability. Give a child or a small group of children a copy of the text and ask them to cut out all the pronouns in the text. Ask them to sort out the pronouns that are masculine, feminine and relating to a person. Give them another text with the pronouns blanked out and ask them to replace them with their cut out pronouns.

The Word ladder

A similar game to 'Consequences'. In groups of four the children are given strips of paper with four sections (see Word ladder Template – Teacher resources). The children write a pronoun on the first section, fold over the paper to hide it and pass it to the next child. They then write another pronoun on the next and so on. After the strip has been completed it is opened up and the children read out the four written pronouns.

They use the pronouns to orally tell a short story or a recount. They could also use them to write a short story or poem.

Singular pronouns

Learning Objectives:
- To understand that a pronoun is a word that takes the place of a noun.

- To recognise and use singular pronouns.

Resources:
- **Lesson** – 'Little Miss Muffet' and 'Singular Pronoun cards 1' (Lesson resources-CD ROM).

- **Group 1** - Scissors, glue, copies of activity sheet 1, 'Little Red Riding Hood' for each child.

- **Group 2** – Copies of activity sheet 2 'Pronoun Tales' for each child. Singular Pronoun word search-(Teacher resources – CD-ROM)

- **Group 3** - Copies of activity sheet 3, 'The Gingerbread Man' for each child.

Lesson/activity notes:
- **Lesson** - Have the pronoun cards on display as the children work on their activities.

- **Group 1** - Children can work individually or in a group on their activity sheets. The group will need adult support.

- **Group 2** – Children work individually on their activity sheet and their word search.

- **Group 3** – Children work individually on their activity sheet and then discuss their work in pairs.

Lesson

Introduction
Display 'Little Miss Muffet', for all the children to see. Read the original rhyme with the children. Point to version 2 and read it out slowly. Ask the children what is different about this version. Some of the children may say *There are lots of Miss Muffets* or *'Miss Muffet' is used instead of the word 'her.'* Ask the children which version sounds better. Why? Underline the word 'her' in the original version. Explain that 'her' is a word called a pronoun which takes the place of a noun to make a sentence sound better

Main lesson
Ask some children to come out and hold up the 'Singular pronoun cards'. Explain that all these words are pronouns and are used to replace single nouns, e.g. one person or an object. Make up a sentence without a pronoun such as 'Grace loves Grace's rabbit'. Ask the children which pronoun could be used instead of Grace and write the sentence on the board, e.g. 'Grace loves her rabbit'

or 'She loves her rabbit'. Once a pronoun is used, put the card down. With the children make up more sentences until all the pronouns are used.

Explain to the children that they are going to do activities with pronouns. Put the children into their levelled groups. Spend time moving between the groups to discuss individual children's work and assess their level of understanding.

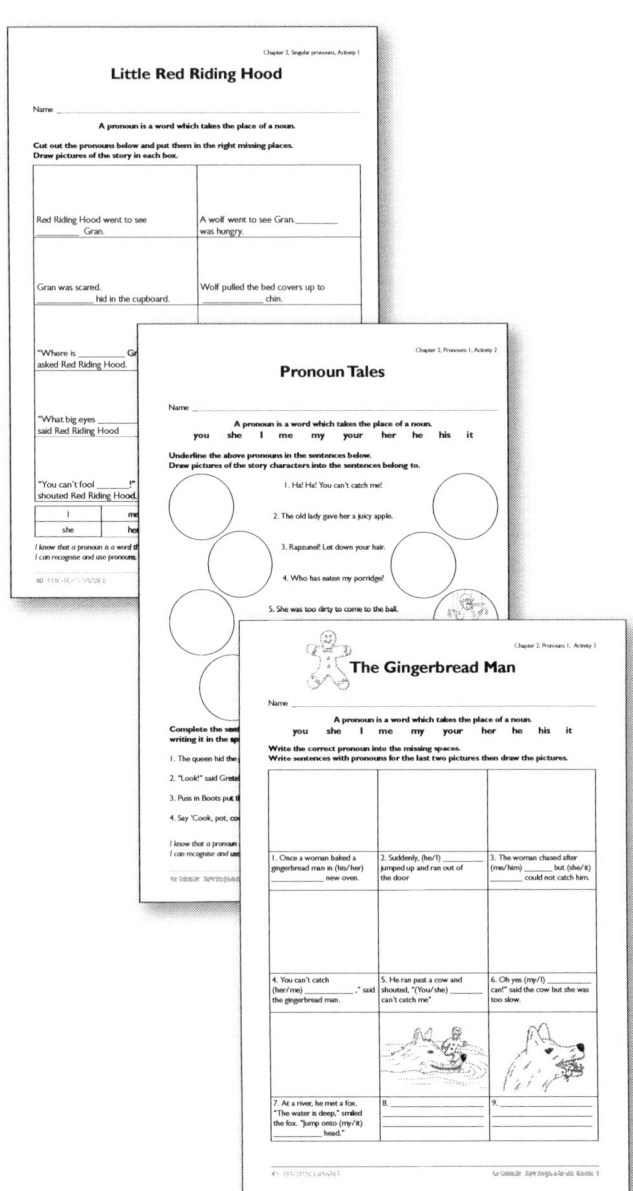

Activities

Group 1
- Give out the copies of activity sheet, 'Little Red Riding Hood' to each of the children.

- Ask the children to cut out the pronouns from the bottom of the page and read them out.

- Go through the story with the children.

- Go back to the first frame and read through the first sentence. Ask them to choose a pronoun to put in the missing space.

- Ask them to read out the sentence. Does it make sense? If it does, let them stick the pronoun into the space.

- Once the story is complete, let the children take turns to read out the story. Let them draw in the pictures.

Group 2

- Give out copies of the activity sheet 'Pronoun Tales' to the children

- Working individually, the children underline pronouns in sentences and draw matching story character.

- Finally they choose the right pronoun for four sentences.

- If time, give the children the singular pronoun word search.

Group 3

- Give out copies of the activity sheet 'The Gingerbread Man,' to the children.

- Working individually the children must write in the correct pronoun to the sentences of a traditional story.

- They then write the last two sentences with pronouns and illustrate the comic strip.

- Once they have completed the activity, ask them to work in pairs and discuss which nouns the pronouns could have replaced. Which text works better? Why?

Plenary

Before the end of the lesson, bring all the groups together. Ask, *'How do you think pronouns make sentences in writing and speaking sound better?'* Encourage them to look at stories and rhymes to see how many pronouns they can spot.

Support:

Choose a story or a nursery rhyme with a simple text and read the story with the children. Point to singular pronouns within the different sentences. With the children add in the noun, that the pronoun replaced and compare the two sentences.

Extension:

Highlight that singular pronouns are words that replace single nouns such as one person or one object. Let the children listen to the lyrics of a song. Ask them to make a tally of how many times they hear a singular pronoun. Give them a copy of the lyrics to highlight and check against their pronoun tally.

Little Red Riding Hood

Name _____

A pronoun is a word which takes the place of a noun.

**Cut out the pronouns below and put them in the right missing places.
Draw pictures of the story in each box.**

Red Riding Hood went to see _____ Gran.	A wolf went to see Gran._____ was hungry.
Gran was scared. _____ hid in the cupboard.	Wolf pulled the bed covers up to _____ chin.
"Where is _____ Gran?" asked Red Riding Hood.	"Here _____ am, dear?" said the wolf.
"What big eyes _____ have, Gran," said Red Riding Hood	All the better to see _____pretty face," smiled the wolf.
"You can't fool _____!" shouted Red Riding Hood.	She kicked the wolf out of bed and chased _____ into woods.

I	me	my	you	your
she	her	he	him	his

I know that a pronoun is a word that takes the place of a noun.
I can recognise and use pronouns.

Pronoun Tales

Name _____

A pronoun is a word which takes the place of a noun.

you   she   I   me   my   your   her   he   his   it

Underline the above pronouns in the sentences below.
Draw pictures of the story characters into the sentences belong to.

1. Ha! Ha! You can't catch me!

2. The old lady gave her a juicy apple.

3. Rapzunel! Let down your hair.

4. Who has eaten my porridge?

5. She was too dirty to come to the ball.

6. Every time he told a lie his nose grew

7. It jumped into grandma's bed.

8. The sky is falling! I must tell the king.

Complete the sentence by choosing the right pronoun in the brackets and writing it in the spaces.

1. The queen hid the pea. The princess did not know _____ (I/it) was there.

2. "Look!" said Gretel. "_____ (My/Her) house is made from sweets.

3. Puss in Boots put the rabbit in the sack. _____ (He/His) gave it to the King.

4. Say 'Cook, pot, cook'. It will give _____ (it/you) hot porridge.

I know that a pronoun is a word that takes the place of a noun.
I can recognise and use pronouns.

The Gingerbread Man

Name _____

A pronoun is a word which takes the place of a noun.

you   she   I   me   my   your   her   he   his   it

Write the correct pronoun into the missing spaces.
Write sentences with pronouns for the last two pictures then draw the pictures.

1. Once a woman baked a gingerbread man in (his/her) _____ new oven.	2. Suddenly, (he/I) _____ jumped up and ran out of the door	3. The woman chased after (me/him) _____ but (she/it) _____ could not catch him.
4. You can't catch (her/me) _____ ," said the gingerbread man.	5. He ran past a cow and shouted, "(You/she) _____ can't catch me"	6. Oh yes (my/I) _____ can!" said the cow but she was too slow.
7. At a river, he met a fox. "The water is deep," smiled the fox. "Jump onto (my/it) _____ head."	8. _____ _____ _____	9. _____ _____ _____

Grammar Springboards Book 1

Plural pronouns

Learning Objectives:
- To understand that a pronoun is a word that takes the place of a noun.

- To recognise and use plural pronouns.

Resources:
- **Lesson** – 'Three Blind Mice' and 'Plural pronoun cards' (Lesson Resources -CD-ROM)

- **Group 1** –A set of 'Plural pronoun cards', a set of activity; Noun space cards', paper and pen or whiteboard for all the group.

- **Group 2** – Copies of activity sheet 2.1, 'Pronoun Blast Off' for each child and activity sheet 2.2., 'Pronoun Blast Off 2' to each pair of children.

- **Group 3** - Copies of activity sheet 3.1, 'Invasion of the Aliens' and activity sheet 3.2, 'Message in Space'.

Lesson/activity notes:
- **Lesson** - Prepare the 'Plural pronoun cards' before the lesson. Use a large computer monitor to show 'Three Blind Mice' and display it for all the class to see.

- **Group 1** - Children work as a discussion group with adult support writing out their sentences

- **Group 2** – Children work individually on activity sheet 2.1 and then in pairs on activity sheet 2.2

- **Group 3** – Children work individually on activity sheet 3.1 and in pairs on activity sheet 3.2.

Lesson

Introduction
Display 'Three blind mice'. With the children read out the first original version. Now slowly read out the second version, pointing to the words at the same time. Ask the children what is different about this version. Some of the children may say *'Three blind mice' is used a lot'*, *'it doesn't rhyme'* or *'there are too many words.'* Underline the words 'Three blind mice' on the second version and ask the children what words have sometimes replaced them in the first version – they, their. Underline the words.

Main lesson
Explain to the children that the words 'they' and 'their' are called pronouns. Explain that a pronoun takes the place of a noun to make a sentence sound better. Highlight that the pronouns 'they' and 'their' replace plural nouns e.g. more than one person or object. Hold up the 'Plural pronoun cards' and with the class, read out each word. Ask the children to think of a sentence using one of the plural pronouns. Write it on the board and read it out.

Write a version without the pronoun. Discuss how the pronoun improves sentence. Go through all the pronouns.

Explain to the children that they are going to investigate plural pronouns set in space. Put the children into their levelled groups. Spend time moving between the groups to discuss individual children's work and assess their level of understanding.

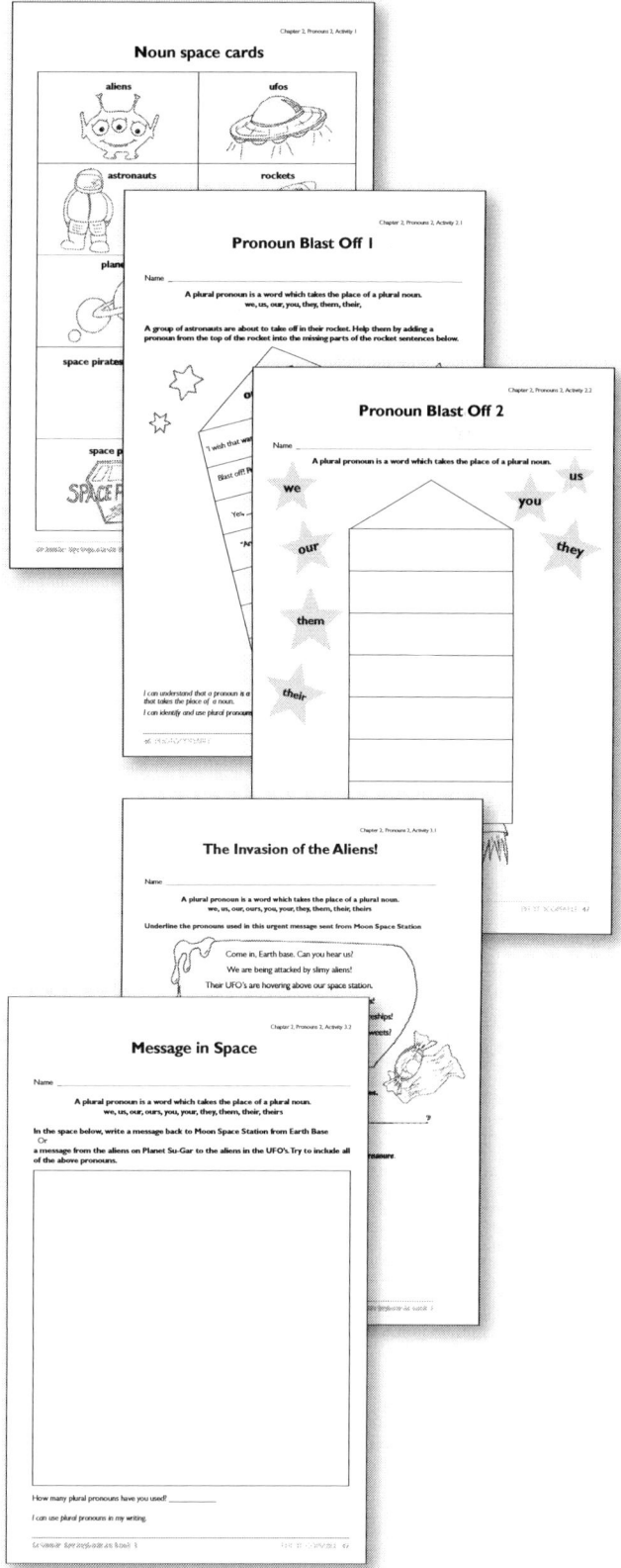

Activities

Group One

- Put one set of the 'Plural pronoun cards' face down in a pile in front of the children.

- Put one set of the 'Noun space cards' face down in a separate pile.

- Let the children take turns to turn over a pronoun card and a picture plural noun.

- Encourage them to create two sentences. The first using the picture noun and the second using the pronoun, e.g. The UFOs were round. They looked pretty.

- Write them out for the children to read or see. Do they make sense?

- Ask the children to circle the plural pronoun. Take note of their knowledge.

Group 2

- Give out copies of activity sheet 'Pronoun Blast Off' to each child.

- Working individually, the children add missing pronouns into seven sentences.

- With the children, discuss how the pronouns improve the sentences.

- Give out the 'Pronoun Blast Off2' sheet and ask the children to work in pairs to write seven simple sentences using the pronouns at the top of the rocket. The sentences don't have to do with space.

- Encourage the children to share their sentences with another pair or within the group.

Group 3

- Give out copies of activity sheet 'Invasion of the Aliens' to each child.

- Working individually, the children underline the pronouns in the astronaut message.

- They then add in the correct pronouns to the alien message.

- Once they have completed the activity, ask the children to work in pairs to write a return message from either Earth Base or Planet Su-Gar using pronouns in their sentences. They can write it on, 'Message in Space' activity sheet.

Plenary

At the end of the lesson, bring the groups together. Encourage the children to read out their pronoun sentences. Ask them what a pronoun word does. Show the plural pronoun cards again and remind the children that these are plural nouns and used to replace nouns that are more than one thing.

Support

For children who need extra support in identifying plural nouns, look at more nursery rhymes and simple poetry and discuss how they would sound without the plural pronouns.

Extension

Give the children a short fiction text and a short non-fiction text. Ask them to record the plural pronouns in each text and how may time each one is used. Discuss their findings. Ask where some pronouns are used more in a non-fiction text and vice versa.

Noun space cards

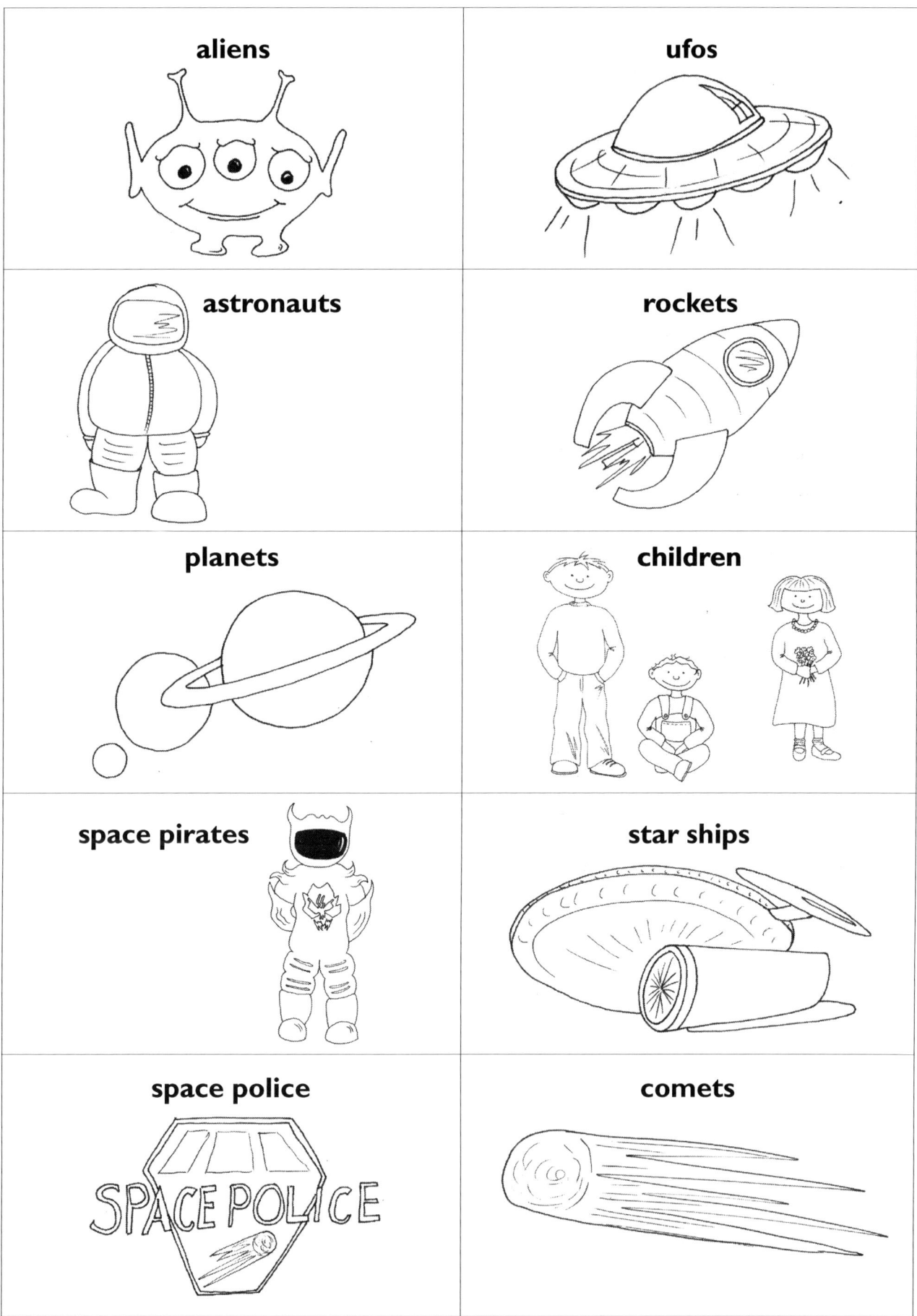

aliens

ufos

astronauts

rockets

planets

children

space pirates

star ships

space police

SPACE POLICE

comets

Pronoun Blast Off 1

Name _____

A plural pronoun is a word which takes the place of a plural noun.
we, us, our, you, they, them, their,

A group of astronauts are about to take off in their rocket. Help them by adding a pronoun from the top of the rocket into the missing parts of the rocket sentences below.

we, us,
our, you, they,
them, their,

'I wish that was _____," say a boy and girl.

Blast off! People watch _____ zoom up into space.

Yes, _____ are," say the astronauts.

"Are _____ all ready for take off?" ask Earth Control.

"We must put _____ seatbelts on," say the astronauts.

_____ shut the rocket door tightly.

The astronauts climb into _____ rocket.

I can understand that a pronoun is a word that takes the place of a noun.

I can identify and use plural pronouns.

Pronoun Blast Off 2

Name _____

A plural pronoun is a word which takes the place of a plural noun.

we

us

you

our

they

them

their

I can use plural pronouns in my writing.

The Invasion of the Aliens!

Name _____

A plural pronoun is a word which takes the place of a plural noun.
we, us, our, ours, you, your, they, them, their, theirs

Underline the pronouns used in this urgent message sent from Moon Space Station

> Come in, Earth base. Can you hear us?
>
> We are being attacked by slimy aliens!
>
> Their UFO's are hovering above our space station.
>
> When we look out of the window, they wave at us!
>
> We don't know how to stop them. Launch all your spaceships!
>
> Come quickly! Could we also have some more moon sweets?
>
> The aliens have eaten all of ours! Over and out!

Complete the alien message by adding pronouns in the missing spaces.

COME IN, PLANET SU-GAR. CAN YOU HEAR _____?

_____ have found the space station.

The Su-Gar radar has found _____ moon sweet treasure.

We have beamed them _____ up.

Slurp! _____ taste delicious.

_____ UFOs are now off to Earth

_____ sweets are so much better

See _____ all there! Over and Slurp!

I can understand that a pronoun is a word that takes the place of a noun.
I can identify and use plural pronouns.

Message in Space

Name _____

A plural pronoun is a word which takes the place of a plural noun.
we, us, our, ours, you, your, they, them, their, theirs

In the space below, write a message back to Moon Space Station from Earth Base
  Or
a message from the aliens on Planet Su-Gar to the aliens in the UFO's. Try to include all of the above pronouns.

How many plural pronouns have you used? _____

I can use plural pronouns in my writing.

Chapter 3 - Verbs

Verb Information

Definition:

- Verbs are words that describe what nouns do.

- Verbs are very important. They form a main part of sentence and give it a reason.

- Verbs bring ideas, events, place, and people together.

- They enhance writing and can be used to great effect.

- Unlike other words, most verbs change in their form.
  E.g. lie, lay, laid.

Main verbs

These verbs describe what something or someone does or is.
- Action verbs: e.g. play, kick, jump, drink, sleep.
  E.g. Katy played with her yo-yo.

- Verbs describing a state. E.g. kind, seem, belong –
  The ball belonged to Joe.

Helping verbs

Helping verbs can be used with main verbs. They have no meaning if used on their own.
We usually use 'helping' verbs with main verbs.
E.g. The children were eating a cake. I am riding my bike.

Helping verbs include:
Being verbs –these helping verbs show that a subject exists
E.g. are, am, is, was, were, been, being, be

- We use 'am' or ''was, if the subject of the sentence is "I"
  - *I am at my nan's. I was at my nan's.*
- We use 'is' or 'was', if the subject of the sentence is singular.
  – *Tim is sick. Tim was sick.*
- We use 'were' or 'are' if the subject of the sentence is plural.
  – *We were tired. We are tired.*

Having verbs – these helping verbs show what a subject has.
E.g. has, have, having, had
Joe has a spot.
Luke is having a bath.
Molly had a bad tooth.

Saying verbs
Saying verbs describe how a subject talks or sounds.
E.g. shout, roar, laugh, cry, whisper, call, say

Singular and plural verbs
Verbs can be singular or plural
The basic rule is:
1. A singular verb is used *with a singular subject*
    E.g. The girl kicks a ball.

2. A plural verb is used with a plural subject.
    E.g. The girls kick a ball

Verb tenses
Definition of tense – a way to tell the difference in time - past, present, future.
Verbs change to show tenses when something happens or happened.

Present tense: what is happening now.

E.g. Liam is drinking apple juice.

Regular present verb – present participle rule
1. Most verbs become present tense by adding –ing to the end of the word,
    E.g. sleep-sleeping, kick-kicking.

2. Regular verbs that end in 'e' must drop the 'e' before adding 'ing'.
    E.g. ride-riding, bake-baking.

Past tense: what has happened.
E.g. I lost my purse when I went shopping.

Regular past verb – past participle rule
1. Most verbs become past tense by adding –ed to the end of the word.
    E.g. jump-jumped, call-called.

2. Regular verbs that end in 'e' must only add 'd' to the end of the word.
    E.g. dance-danced, like- liked.

Future tense: what is about to happen

Sara is going to see her friend next week.

Regular and Irregular verbs
Regular verbs: Most verbs which follow the simple past participle and present participle rules when changes tenses.
E.g. look, looked, looking.

Irregular verbs: The verbs change spelling in the past tense and past participle. There are no definite rules so they need to be learnt.
E.g. buy, bought, brought, go, went, saw, see.

Verb Springboards

Word Walls

Create eye catching word walls. One flash card equals one brick. Have several bricks to create the word wall with the children. Have blank cards that the children can write new verbs and add to or make a new word wall shape. Use them as games with the children e.g. sorting the words into right pairs.

The walls can be used in a variety of ways.

- Action verbs – action verbs in categories e.g. sports, hobbies.

- Saying verbs- different saying verbs that could replace 'said'.

- Past tense verbs – pairs of base verbs with 'ed' ending words or base words with 'd' ending verbs.

- Present tense verbs – pairs of base verbs with ing verbs.

- Irregular pairs of verbs.

The Word ladder

A similar game to 'Consequences'. In groups of four the children are given strips of paper with four sections (see Word ladder Template – Teacher resources). The children write a verb on the first section, fold over the paper to hide it and pass it to the next child. They then write another verb on the next and so on. After the strip has been completed it is opened up and the children read out the four written verbs.

- The game can be used for action verbs where the children create a short story sequence or recount using the verbs or making simple sentences. Saying verbs- the children use the saying verbs to create speaking characters.

Word wheel/ Word slide

(see Teacher resources for templates)

The teacher or children add verbs to the wheels or slides to explore how verbs change when they become simple past and present tense verbs. Also a good reinforcement resource.

Missing verbs

Make copies of a fictional or non-fictional text and blank out the verbs (could be all or specific such as saying verbs, past tense –ed verbs). Give copies to a group of children and ask them to list the verbs that they think are missing. Compare the verb lists with the other groups.

Story telling circle

Each child is given or told a saying verb. A story is started with a dialogue sentence. The next children in the circle add their own dialogue sentence to the story in the verbal expression of their saying verb.

Other activity ideas

- Listen and look at the lyrics of action rhymes, e.g. Here we go round the Mulberry Bush, London's Burning, and Farmer's in his den.

- Play action game such as 'Simon says...' or O'Grady says...' Adapt it to saying verbs and the children have to say a set sentence in the style of the saying verb.

- Alphabet verb lists.

- Children writing explanatory texts of a topic highlighting present tense 'ing' verbs.

- The children draw pin people or verb badges to go with action verbs.

- Creating or solving word searches, solving puzzles.

- Ten minute challenge to make a list of as many verbs as possible. Categories include action verbs, saying verbs, past or present tense verbs or irregular pairs of verbs.

- Take photos of the children doing something. Print them and turn them into a verb book with sentence captions under each picture. Highlight the verbs.

- Create displays of verb categories with labels and captions. For example draw large outlines of a boy and girl and show the verbs related to the body- sniff, run, and sneeze. Have pockets of labels to show the past, present tense version of each verb.

- Create antonym and synonym verbs displays. Use mobiles or 3D models to encourage the children to look at the words.

- Speech bubble fun. Use the speech bubble templates or make your own. Ask the children in groups or pairs to write a dialogue sentence spoken in the style of a given saying verb.

Action verbs

Learning Objectives:

- To understand that a verb shows what something or someone does.

- To understand that some verbs describe actions.

- To identify and use action verbs.

Resources:

- **Lesson** - 'The Word Web' template if needed.-(Teacher resources-CD ROM)

- **Group 1** - Copies of activity sheet 1 'Sports' for each child.

- **Group 2** - Copies of activity sheet 2, 'Hobbies' for each child. Copies of 'The Word Web' for each pair of children.

- **Group 3** - Copies of activity sheet 3, 'Action verbs word search' for each child.

Lesson/activity notes

- **Lesson** – Make sure the children are away from the furniture when playing 'Simon says'.

- **Group 1** – Children work as a discussion group with adult support.

- **Group 2** – Children work individually and then in pairs. The group may need adult support

- **Group 3** – Children work individually and then pair-share word searches.

Lesson

Introduction

Play the game 'Simon says' with all the class. Choose action verbs such as, 'Simon says...run, jump, skip, hop, march etc.' Finish the game with the action verb 'sit'. Once all the children have sat down, explain that all the action words are called verbs. Say that verbs are words that show what something or someone does. Write the verbs used in the game. Explain that these verbs are called action verbs as they show different actions.

Main lesson

Draw a verb web on the board (see 'The Word Web' template) and write the title 'Action verbs' in the middle. Add an action verb. Ask each child for an example of an action verb and add it to the web, e.g. walk, jump, crawl, ski. Once the action verb web is full, explain that they are going to make an action verb list poem. Start by writing a simple line with your verb e.g. Charlie likes to crawl on his knees. Highlight the alliteration and the verb. Let the children say their action verb sentences and write them on the board as a list, e.g. Joe likes to jump in the air. Read out the action verb list poem with the children.

Explain to the children that they are going to do action verb activities. Put the children into their levelled groups and give out the activities. Spend time moving between the groups to discuss individual children's work and assess their level of understanding.

Activities

Group 1

- Give out copies of the activity sheet, 'Sports' to each of the children.

- As a discussion group, go through the pictures with the children and ask what sport they represent. Highlight how each picture shows an action.

- Read through the action verbs at the side and ask the children to link the right action verb to the right sport.

- Encourage each of the children to draw a picture of a sport and help them if needed write the action verb underneath the picture.

Group 2:

- Give out copies of the activity sheet 'Hobbies' to each child.

- Discuss with the children their favourite hobbies. Highlight action verbs used in the hobbies, e.g. play, knit, kick.

- Working individually, the children underline the action verbs in sentences about hobbies.

- They then add a few more action verbs to a word web on hobbies and use the web to add the missing action verbs into three sentences.

- If time, put the children in pairs and give them a blank copy of 'The Word Web'. Ask them to list action verbs for their favourite hobby. How many verbs can they list?

Group 3:

- Give each child a copy of activity sheet 3, 'Action verbs word search'.

- Working individually, the children complete the word search verb list by adding five more action verbs.

- The children then incorporate the verbs into the word search grid.

- Once they have done that ask them to choose two of the action verbs and write two sentences using the verbs.

- Let the children swap their word searches with each other to solve and discuss the verbs used.

Plenary:

Before the end of the lesson, bring all the groups back together. Ask the children for examples of action verbs they have been working on. Ask the children what an action verb is – an action or doing word. If time, play a game of action verb charades- Choose one or two children to mime an action verb for the class to guess.

Support:

To give children more support on action verbs, help them create a simple comic strip recount of a journey, a game, or an activity that they have experienced. With the children write simple sentences underneath each picture frame with an action verb.

Extension:

Encourage the children to read a short adventure story and record the action verbs used in the text. Discuss how the action verbs make the story exciting. Suggest they create and act out an adventure sequence using different actions and get others to guess the verbs.

Sports

Name _____

Verbs are words that show what something or someone does.

Draw a line to match the verb with the right sport.

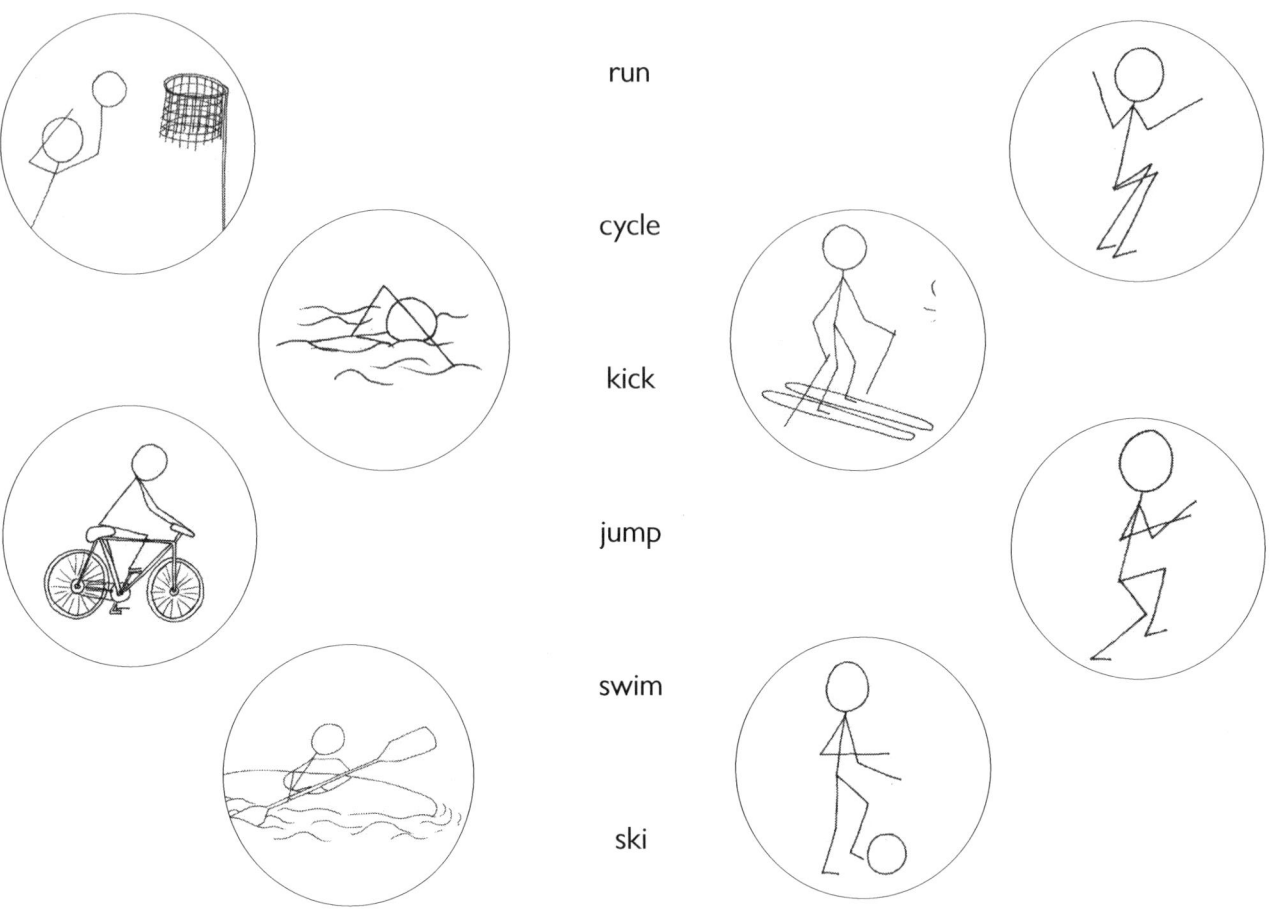

run

cycle

kick

jump

swim

ski

Draw a picture of an action verb in the box below. Write the verb on the line.

_____

I can understand that verbs describe actions
I can identify action verbs. .

Hobbies

Name _____

Verbs are words that show what something or someone does.

Underline the action verbs in these sentences.

1. Joel likes to play the piano

3. Mrs West likes to knit.

5. Daisy likes to kick a football.

2. Mia likes to dance.

4. Mr Troy likes to paint.

6. Ahmed likes to sing.

This word web shows action verbs used in hobbies.
Can you add any more verbs to the web?

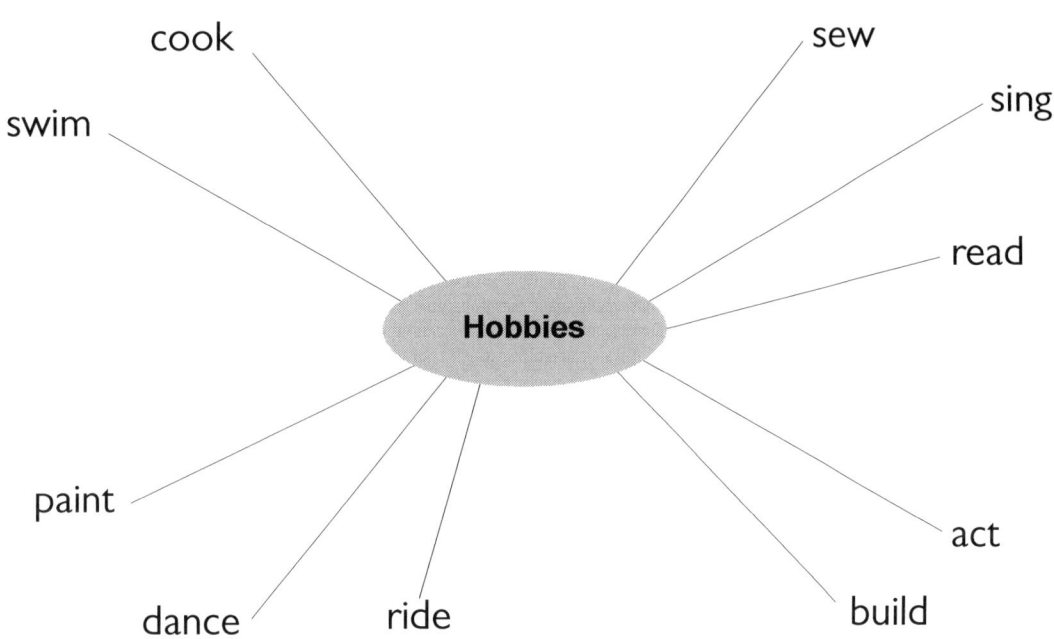

Use the web to fill in the missing action verbs in the three sentences below.

Joe went to the stables to _____ his pony.

Zoe loves to _____ chocolate cake.

I like to sit on my bed and _____ a book

I can understand that verbs can describe actions.
I can identify and use action verbs.

Action verbs Word Search

Name _____

Verbs are words that show what something or someone does.

Write five more action verbs to the word search list below. Add all the action verbs into the word search grid. They can go across, down, or diagonally. Once the verbs are added in, fill the rest of the grid with letters.

d						p			
	a					a			
		n			s	i	n	g	
						n			
			c			t			
				e					
				m					
			i						
		w				f	i	s	h
	s								

Action verb words

1. dance   2. paint   3. sing   4. swim   5. fish

6. _____ 7. _____ 8. _____ 9. _____ 10. _____

Choose two action verbs and use them to write two sentences below.

_____

_____

I can understand that verbs can describe actions.
I can identify and use action verbs.

'Saying' verbs

Learning Objectives:
- To understand that a saying verb' is a word that tells you how someone talks.

- To identify and use saying verbs.

Resources:
- **Lesson:** 'The Lion Dance 1' and 'The Lion Dance 2'– (Lesson resources –CD ROM).

- **Group 1:-** One copy of activity sheet 1, 'Saying verb characters'. Large paper speech bubbles to write words inside- ('Speech bubble' template-teacher resources- CD-ROM).

- **Group 2** –Copies of activity sheet 2, 'Which saying verb?' for each child.

- **Group 3:** Copy of activity sheet 3.1, 'Saying word web' and an activity sheet 3.2, 'The Hare and the Tortoise' for each pair of children thesaurus, word bank.

Lesson/activity notes
- **Group 1:** Children work as a discussion group with an adult. Record their responses and choices during the activity.

- **Group 2:** Children work individually and then in pairs.

- **Group 3:** Children work in pairs and then individually.

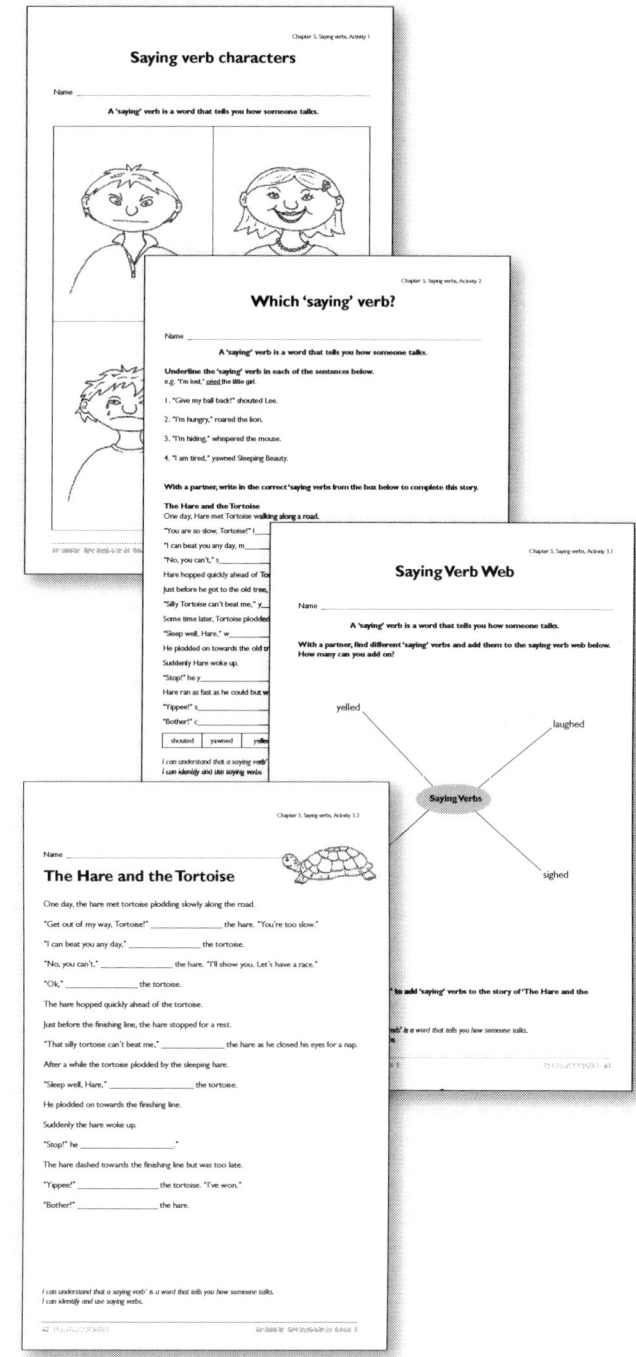

Lesson

Introduction
Revise the meaning of a verb. Highlight that one type of verb is a 'saying' verb-a word that tells you how someone is talking. Give an example e.g. 'Where are you?' whispered Sam. Put the children into groups of three and give each group a 'saying' verb (either on a piece of paper or whispered), e.g. cry, groan, whisper, gasp. Ask each group to say 'Where are you?' in the style of their 'saying' verb and ask the rest of the groups what they think the 'saying' verb is.

Main lesson
Highlight how 'saying' verbs can be used to make a story more interesting. Read 'The Lion Dance 1' to the children. Ask the children to listen out for any 'saying' verbs. Read through the text and ask the children if they heard any 'saying' verbs. Some may say just 'said.' Read another version of the story with more 'saying' verbs. Ask the children to listen and put their hand up when they hear them. At the end of the story ask the children for the 'saying' verbs and list them on the board. Discuss how 'saying' verbs help show how the characters talk.

Explain to the children that they are going to do 'saying' verb activities. Put the children into their levelled groups and give out the activities. Spend time moving between the groups to discuss individual children's work and assess their level of understanding

Activities

Group 1
- Working as a discussion group, show the children the pictures of four characters from activity sheet 1.

- Encourage the children to discuss who the characters might be.

- Put a speech bubble shape above a character and ask each child to give an example of 'saying' verb that would describe how the character would talk.

- Write their saying verb suggestions in the speech bubble, e.g. sob, cry, shout, yell.

- Encourage the children to choose one 'saying' verb from the speech bubble and use it in a spoken sentence, e.g. *'I want my rattle,'* howled the little prince.

- Follow the same procedure with each character.

Group 2:
- Give out copies of the activity sheet 'Which 'saying' verb?' to the children.

- Working individually, the children identify and underline the 'saying' verbs in a set of sentences.

- They then work in pairs to complete a short story by adding in missing 'saying verbs' from a choice listed on the sheet.

- Ask them to read through the story. Ask, *'Does it make sense?' Have you chosen the right saying verb for the character?'*

- If time, encourage the children to work in two's or threes to orally make up a short story using 'saying' verbs.

Group 3:
- Put the children into pairs and give each pair a copy of 'Saying verb web'. Leave out copies of a simple thesaurus or the 'saying' verb word list from the Word Bank.

- Working in pairs, the children collect and record as many 'saying' verbs that they can use to replace the 'said' verb.

- Once they have completed the web, give the pair a copy of 'The Hare and the Tortoise'.

- Ask them to use their webs to add in better 'saying' verbs than 'said' in the story.

- Once they have finished, encourage the children to share their story with the group.

- Ask: *How have the different 'saying' verbs improved the story? How do they help us understand what the characters are like?*

Plenary:
At the end of the lesson, bring the groups together. Ask: *'How do saying verbs help a reader or listen of stories and poems?'* 'Saying' verbs show what a character or characters are feeling and how they talk.

Support:
Ask the child to orally think of a saying word and write the word in their text or spell it out. Praise the child for using an adventurous word. When they are telling a story encourage the use of saying words.

Extension:
Encourage the children to be more adventurous with their saying verbs in their own writing. Show them examples from story books or rhymes and poems and highlight the use of alliteration and onomatopoeia, e.g. *'Just one apple, my dear'* cackled the crone. *'Food! Gobbled the goose.'*

Saying verb characters

Name _____

A 'saying' verb is a word that tells you how someone talks.

Which 'saying' verb?

Name _____

A 'saying' verb is a word that tells you how someone talks.

Underline the 'saying' verb in each of the sentences below.
e.g. "I'm lost," <u>cried</u> the little girl.

1. "Give my ball back!" shouted Lee.

2. "I'm hungry," roared the lion.

3. "I'm hiding," whispered the mouse.

4. "I am tired," yawned Sleeping Beauty.

With a partner, write in the correct 'saying verbs from the box below to complete this story.

The Hare and the Tortoise
One day, Hare met Tortoise walking along a road.

"You are so slow, Tortoise!" l_____ the hare.

"I can beat you any day, m_____ Tortoise.

"No, you can't," s_____ Hare. "Let's race to that old tree"

Hare hopped quickly ahead of Tortoise.

Just before he got to the old tree, Hare stopped for a rest.

"Silly Tortoise can't beat me," y_____ Hare. "I'll have a quick nap."

Some time later, Tortoise plodded by Hare.

"Sleep well, Hare," w_____ Tortoise.

He plodded on towards the old tree.

Suddenly Hare woke up.

"Stop!" he y_____".

Hare ran as fast as he could but was too late.

"Yippee!" s_____ Tortoise. "I've won."

"Bother!" c_____ Hare

| shouted | yawned | yelled | whispered | laughed | cried | sneered | muttered |

I can understand that a saying verb' is a word that tells you how someone talks.
I can identify and use saying verbs

Saying Verb Web

Name _____

A 'saying' verb is a word that tells you how someone talks.

With a partner, find different 'saying' verbs and add them to the saying verb web below. How many can you add on?

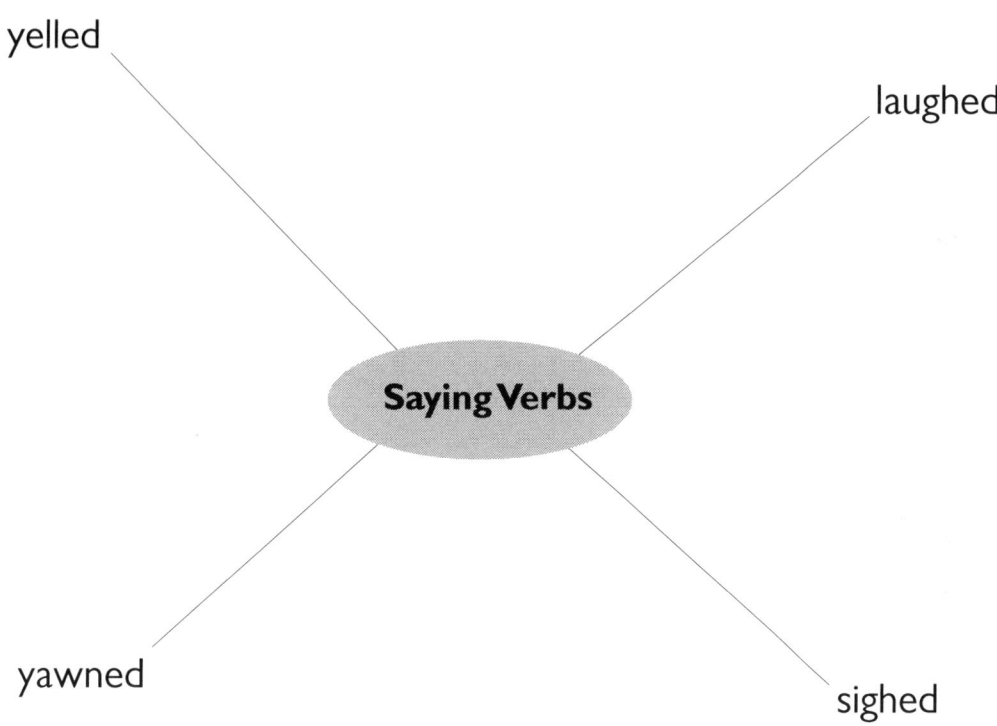

yelled

laughed

Saying Verbs

yawned

sighed

Use your 'Saying verb web' to add 'saying' verbs to the story of 'The Hare and the Tortoise.'

I can understand that a 'saying verb' is a word that tells you how someone talks.
I can identify and use saying verbs.

Name _____

The Hare and the Tortoise

One day, the hare met tortoise plodding slowly along the road.

"Get out of my way, Tortoise!" _____ the hare. "You're too slow."

"I can beat you any day," _____ the tortoise.

"No, you can't," _____ the hare. "I'll show you. Let's have a race."

"Ok," _____ the tortoise.

The hare hopped quickly ahead of the tortoise.

Just before the finishing line, the hare stopped for a rest.

"That silly tortoise can't beat me," _____ the hare as he closed his eyes for a nap.

After a while the tortoise plodded by the sleeping hare.

"Sleep well, Hare," _____ the tortoise.

He plodded on towards the finishing line.

Suddenly the hare woke up.

"Stop!" he _____."

The hare dashed towards the finishing line but was too late.

"Yippee!" _____ the tortoise. "I've won."

"Bother!" _____ the hare.

I can understand that a saying verb' is a word that tells you how someone talks.
I can identify and use saying verbs.

Simple past tense verbs ending in '-ed' or '-d'

Learning Objectives:

- To understand that verbs can describe actions that happens in the past.

- To change simple verb into past tense by adding 'ed' or 'd' if the verb ends in 'e'.

- To recognise and use simple past tense verbs ending in 'ed' and 'd'.

Resources:

- **Lesson** - 'Verb cards 1', 'Verb cards 2', 'ed' and 'd' cards, 'Nothing Much' –(Lesson resources –CD-ROM)

- **Group 1** - One copy of activity sheet 1, 'Past tense verb card activity' to be turned into cards. Two tins or small boxes with 'ed' on one and 'd' on the other.

- **Group 2** –Copies of activity sheet 2, 'Past tense verbs ending in 'ed' and 'd' for each child.

- **Group 3** - Copies of activity sheet 3 'Past tense verbs' for each child.

Lesson/activity notes

- **Group 1** - Children work as a discussion group with an adult.

- **Group 2** - Children work individually and then in pairs.

- **Group 3** - Children work individually.

Lesson

Introduction

Draw a table with the headings of the seven days of the week written down the side. Display the 'Verb cards 1' and 2 for the children to see. Highlight that they are verbs. Explain that most verbs can show actions in the past by adding 'ed' onto their end. Put the 'ed' card next to 'Verb cards 1' and read out each past tense verb. Point to 'Verb Cards 2' and highlight that these verbs all end with 'e' so the children only need to add 'd' onto the end. Put the 'd' card next to the verbs and with the children read out each past tense verb.

Main lesson

Read the story 'Nothing Much' to the children. Write a few of the past tense verbs on the board, e.g. chased, climbed. Underline the 'ed' and 'd' on the verbs. Say that as a class the children are going to create a fun recount of a week by turning the verb cards into past actions. Starting on Monday, show the first verb card and ask if it should have an 'ed' or 'd' on the end. Ask the children for an activity and write their ideas as sentences. Once the activity is completed, read through the story with the children and underline the past tense verbs.

Explain to the children that they are going to do activities using verbs showing past actions. Put the children into their levelled groups and give out the activities. Spend time moving between the groups to discuss individual children's work and assess their level of understanding.

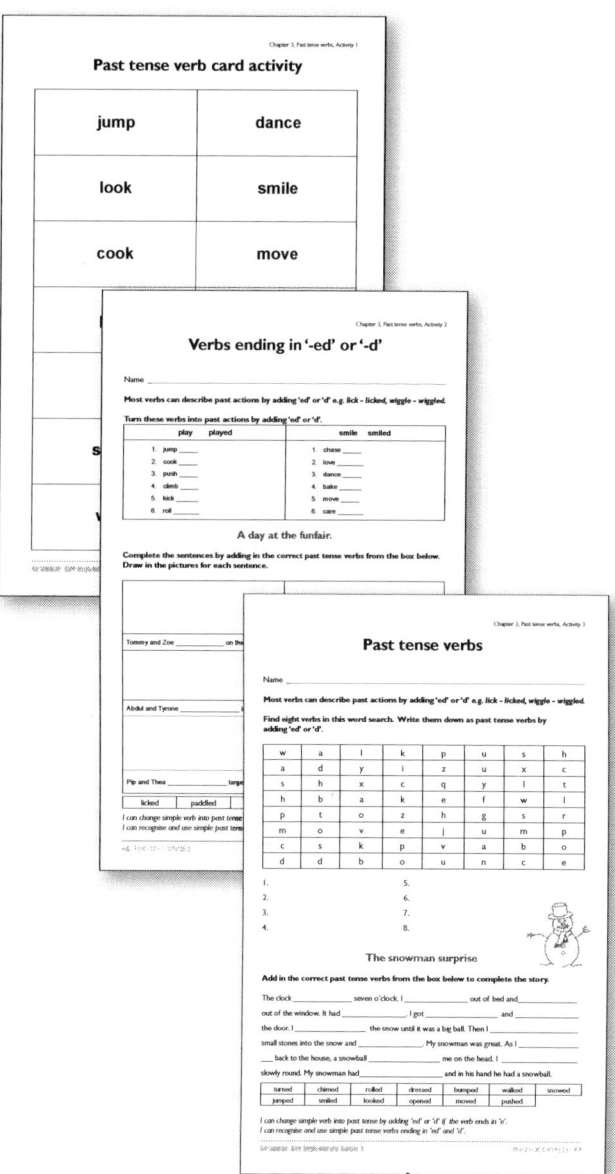

Activities

Group 1

- Put out the two tins or boxes and the shuffled verb cards face down on the table.

- Working as a group, the children take turns to pick up a verb card and read it out.

- Ask the children what the verb is as a past action, e.g. 'rain' becomes 'rained'.

- Ask what they need to add onto the end of the verb to make it a past action 'ed' or 'd' and then put it in the correct tin.

- Once all the cards are in the tins, empty them out and go through each verb reinforcing the endings.

- In pairs ask the children to create an oral recount of a special day such as day trip or a birthday using some of the verbs.

Group 2:

- Give out copies of the activity sheet 2 'Past tense verbs ending in 'ed' and 'd' ' to the children.

- Working individually, the children change two lists of verbs into past tense by adding 'ed' or 'd'.

- They then complete six sentences that show six activities at a fair by adding in missing 'verbs' from a choice listed on the sheet.

- Once the children have completed the sheet, the children can draw in the activities.

Group 3:

- Give out copies of the activity sheet 3, 'Past tense verbs,' to each of the children.

- The children have to solve the word search puzzle and then turn the verbs into past tense by adding 'ed' or 'd'.

- They then complete a fictional recount by adding in the correct past tense verbs.

- Once the children have completed the fictional recount, ask the children to work in pairs to create oral recounts of a special event or a surprise event.

- Encourage the children to retell their recounts to the other pairs in their group and ask them to make notes of past tense verbs.

Plenary:

At the end of the lesson, bring the groups together and discuss their various activities. Write the verb, 'jump' on the board and ask the children what they need to add to the word to make it a past action or past tense. They should say 'ed'. Write the verb, 'move' on the board and ask the children what they need to add to the word to make it a past action or past tense. They should say 'just 'd' as e is already there.

Support:

Use a simple reading text or recount such as a traditional tale and help the children find verbs that end in 'ed' and 'd'. Write them out on a white board and ask the children to underline the 'ed' or 'd' of each verb.

Extension:

Encourage the children to write their own recounts of something they have done in the past. Encourage them to make a word bank of the past tense 'ed' verbs that they come across or use. Highlight that some past tense verbs do not follow simple rules such as saw-see.

Past tense verb card activity

jump	dance
look	smile
cook	move
play	wiped
pull	chase
shout	sneeze
walk	tickle

Verbs ending in '-ed' or '-d'

Name _____

Most verbs can describe past actions by adding 'ed' or 'd' e.g. *lick - licked, wiggle - wiggled*.

Turn these verbs into past actions by adding 'ed' or 'd'.

play played	smile smiled
1. jump _____	1. chase _____
2. cook _____	2. love _____
3. push _____	3. dance _____
4. climb _____	4. bake _____
5. kick _____	5. move _____
6. roll _____	6. care _____

A day at the funfair.

Complete the sentences by adding in the correct past tense verbs from the box below. Draw in the pictures for each sentence.

Tommy and Zoe _____ on the trampoline.	Sarah and Johnny _____ the wall tower.
Abdul and Tyrone _____ in a row boat.	Keira and Mel _____ on the Ghost Train.
Pip and Thea _____ large ice creams.	Charlie and Alfie _____ each other in the dodgem cars.

licked	paddled	bounced	chased	screamed	climbed

I can change simple verb into past tense by adding 'ed' or 'd' if the verb ends in 'e'.
I can recognise and use simple past tense verbs ending in 'ed' and 'd'.

Past tense verbs

Name _____

Most verbs can describe past actions by adding 'ed' or 'd' e.g. *lick – licked, wiggle – wiggled*.

Find eight verbs in this word search. Write them down as past tense verbs by adding 'ed' or 'd'.

w	a	l	k	p	u	s	h
a	d	y	i	z	u	x	c
s	h	x	c	q	y	l	t
h	b	a	k	e	f	w	l
p	t	o	z	h	g	s	r
m	o	v	e	j	u	m	p
c	s	k	p	v	a	b	o
d	d	b	o	u	n	c	e

1.   5.

2.   6.

3.   7.

4.   8.

The snowman surprise

Add in the correct past tense verbs from the box below to complete the story.

The clock _____ seven o'clock. I _____ out of bed and_____

out of the window. It had _____. I got _____ and _____

the door. I _____ the snow until it was a big ball. Then I _____

small stones into the snow and _____. My snowman was great. As I _____

___ back to the house, a snowball _____ me on the head. I _____

slowly round. My snowman had_____ and in his hand he had a snowball.

turned	chimed	rolled	dressed	bumped	walked	snowed
jumped	smiled	looked	opened	moved	pushed	

I can change simple verb into past tense by adding 'ed' or 'd' if the verb ends in 'e'.
I can recognise and use simple past tense verbs ending in 'ed' and 'd'.

Simple present tense verbs ending with '–ing'

Learning Objectives:

• To change a regular verb into present tense by adding '-ing'

• To understand that when '-ing' is added to verbs ending in 'e'. the 'e' is dropped.

• To recognise and use simple present tense verbs ending with '–ing'.

Resources:

• **Lesson** – 'ing'verb machine template '-ing verb slide list', 'ing slide strips' – (Lesson resources.-CD-ROM)

• **Group 1** – A variety of photos/pictures of action verbs for simple –ing rules, e.g. pull, jump, walk. Colouring pens, paper for labels.

• **Group 2** – Copies of activity sheet 1, 'Match the –ing verbs' for each child.

• **Group 3** – Copies of activity sheet 2.1, activity templates 2.2.and 2.3 (can be copied onto card) for each child. Cut out templates for the children to use. Butterfly clips, scissors (if children are doing own templates). Blank wheel template – (Teacher resources CD-ROM)

Lesson/activity notes

• **Lesson** - Before the lesson cut out and create the 'ing verb machine'. Copy or make the two card strips. Have a copy of the 'ing' verb slide lists' near you.

• **Group 1:** Children work as a discussion group with an adult. Record their responses and choices during the activity.

• **Group 2:** Children work individually and then in pairs.

• **Group 3:** Children work individually. Children may need adult support when using the –ing word wheels.

Lesson

Introduction

Put the children into groups of twos or threes. Explain that they are going to play a game using verbs. Highlight how verbs can tell us when things are happening in the past, the future and the present. Explain that the present is what is happening now. Ask *'What is happening now?'* The children could answer, *'We are listening,' 'You are talking.'* Highlight how the children were adding 'ing' to the end of the present tense verbs.

Main lesson

Give each group a verb from the '-ing verb slide lists'. Explain that each group must act out the verb action for the rest of the class to guess. When the class have guessed the action write the verb

on the appropriate strip of card for all the children to see (Strip 1=verbs ending without an 'e', Strip 2=verbs with an 'e' ending.) Show the 'ing verb machine' and point to the 'ing'. Thread in Strip 1 and pull the strip and with the children say out the words. Show Strip 2 and highlight that all these verbs end with e. Explain that when adding -ing to a verb which ends in e, they must drop the e'. Use a pen to cross out the 'e's and pull the strip through the ing machine. Read out the verbs.

Explain to the children that they are going to do activities with –ing verbs. Put the children into their levelled groups and give out the activities. Spend time moving between the groups to discuss individual children's work and assess their level of understanding.

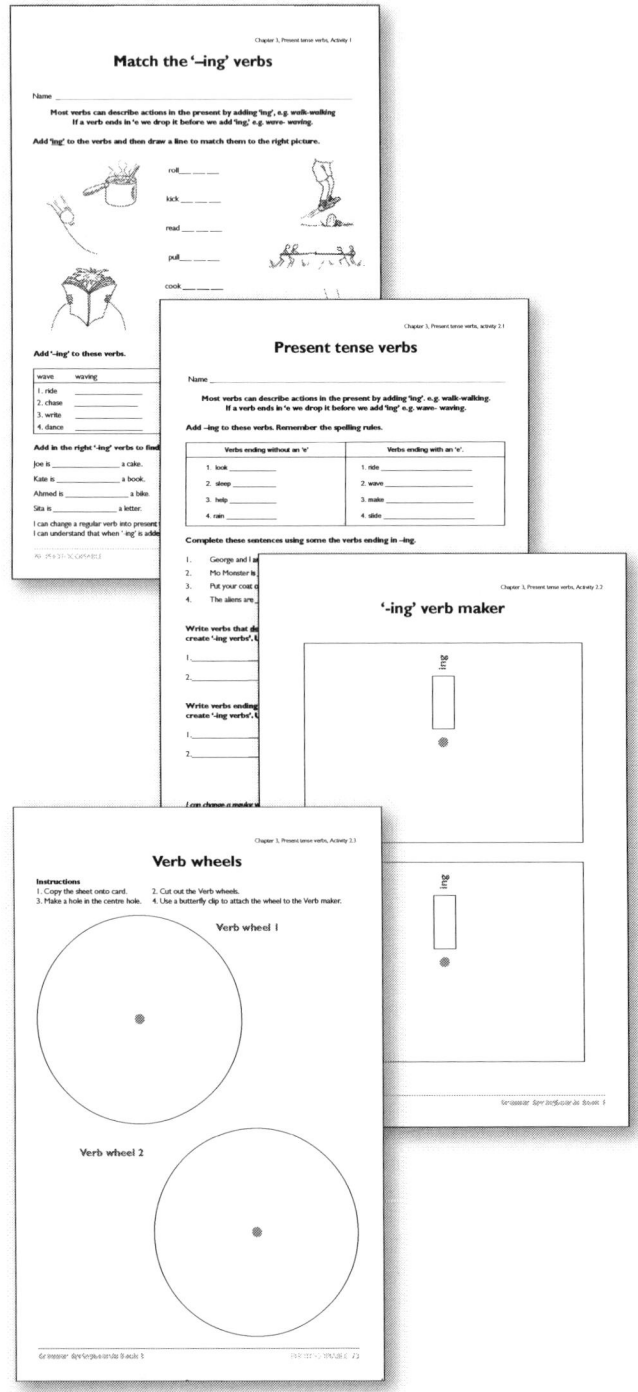

Activities

Group 1

- With the children cut out pictures /photos from magazines to show different verb actions.

- On paper, create labels of the base verb under the relevant pictures/photos, e.g. jump, walk, smile.

- With the children sort out the labels into piles of verbs that end in 'e' and verbs that don't end in 'e.

- Look at verbs which don't end in 'e' and write 'ing' on the end of one.

- Encourage the children to take turns to write 'ing' on the rest of the verbs.

- Look at the pile of verbs ending in 'e'. Show by example the rule of cutting 'e to ad ing. Ask the children to add ing to the rest of these verbs.

- Ask the children to choose one of the verbs from each pile and draw their own pictures of the verbs. Encourage them to write their own labels.

Group 2:

- Give the children copies of the activity sheet 1, 'Match the –ing verbs.'

- Working individually, the children add 'ing' to verbs that do not end in 'e' and then match the verbs to the right pictures showing the verb actions.

- They then add 'ing' to four verbs ending in 'e'.

- They complete the activity sheet by using some of the verbs to complete four sentences.

- At the end of the activity, go over the verbs to reinforce the children's learning.

- If time give them the template of 'ing verb machine' and strips to find more 'ing' verbs.

Group 3:

- Give the children copies of the activity sheet 2.1, Word wheel templates 2.2 and 2.3, butterfly clips and scissors (if children are making the templates).

- Working individually, the children must add –ing to verbs that end with 'e' and verbs that do not end with 'e'.

- They then use some of the –ing verbs to complete five sentences.

- The children then use the –ing verb maker to find –ing verbs and write sentences with them in it.

- If time, let the children create their own –ing verb wheels using a blank wheel template and ask a partner to make sentences.

Plenary:

Before the end of the lesson, bring the groups together and ask them to give examples of verbs that end in 'ing'. Ask the children what they must do to verbs which end in 'e' before they add in 'ing' Write their examples on the board.

Support:

For those children that need more support, create a word bank of verbs that end in ing and those that have an 'e' taken off before an ing. Encourage the children to draw pictures to go with each verb.

Extension:

Encourage the children to find more ing verbs and encourage them to create poster word lists which they can add to as they identify and discover more regular present verbs.

Match the '–ing' verbs

Name _____

Most verbs can describe actions in the present by adding 'ing', e.g. *walk-walking*
If a verb ends in 'e we drop it before we add 'ing,' e.g. *wave- waving.*

Add '<u>ing</u>' to the verbs and then draw a line to match them to the right picture.

roll___ ___ ___

kick ___ ___ ___

read ___ ___ ___

pull___ ___ ___

cook ___ ___ ___

jump ___ ___ ___

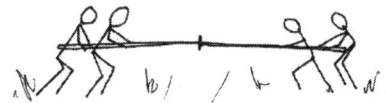

Add '–ing' to these verbs.

wave	waving
1. ride	_____
2. chase	_____
3. write	_____
4. dance	_____

Add in the right '-ing' verbs to find out what Joe and his friends are doing.

Joe is _____ a cake.

Kate is _____ a book.

Ahmed is _____ a bike.

Sita is _____ a letter.

I can change a regular verb into present tense by adding '-ing'.
I can understand that when '-ing' is added to verbs ending in 'e', the 'e' is dropped.

Present tense verbs

Name _____

Most verbs can describe actions in the present by adding 'ing'. e.g. walk-walking.
If a verb ends in 'e we drop it before we add 'ing' e.g. wave- waving.

Add –ing to these verbs. Remember the spelling rules.

Verbs ending without an 'e'	Verbs ending with an 'e'.
1. look _____	1. ride _____
2. sleep _____	2. wave _____
3. help _____	3. make _____
4. rain _____	4. slide _____

Complete these sentences using some the verbs ending in –ing.

1.   George and I are _____ for my ball.

2.   Mo Monster is _____ her mum a special present.

3.   Put your coat on. It is _____.

4.   The aliens are _____ at us from their UFO.

Write verbs that <u>don't</u> end in 'e' onto 'Verbs wheel 1'. Put it in the '-ing verb maker' to create '-ing verbs'. Use two of the -ing verbs to write two sentences below.

1._____

2._____

Write verbs ending with an 'e' onto 'Verbs wheel 2'. Put it in the '-ing verb maker' to create '-ing verbs'. Use two of the -ing verbs to write two sentences below.

1._____

2._____

I can change a regular verb into present tense by adding '-ing'.
I can understand that when '-ing' is added to verbs ending in 'e', the 'e' is dropped.

'-ing' verb maker

ing

ing

Verb wheels

Instructions

1. Copy the sheet onto card.
2. Cut out the Verb wheels.
3. Make a hole in the centre hole.
4. Use a butterfly clip to attach the wheel to the Verb maker.

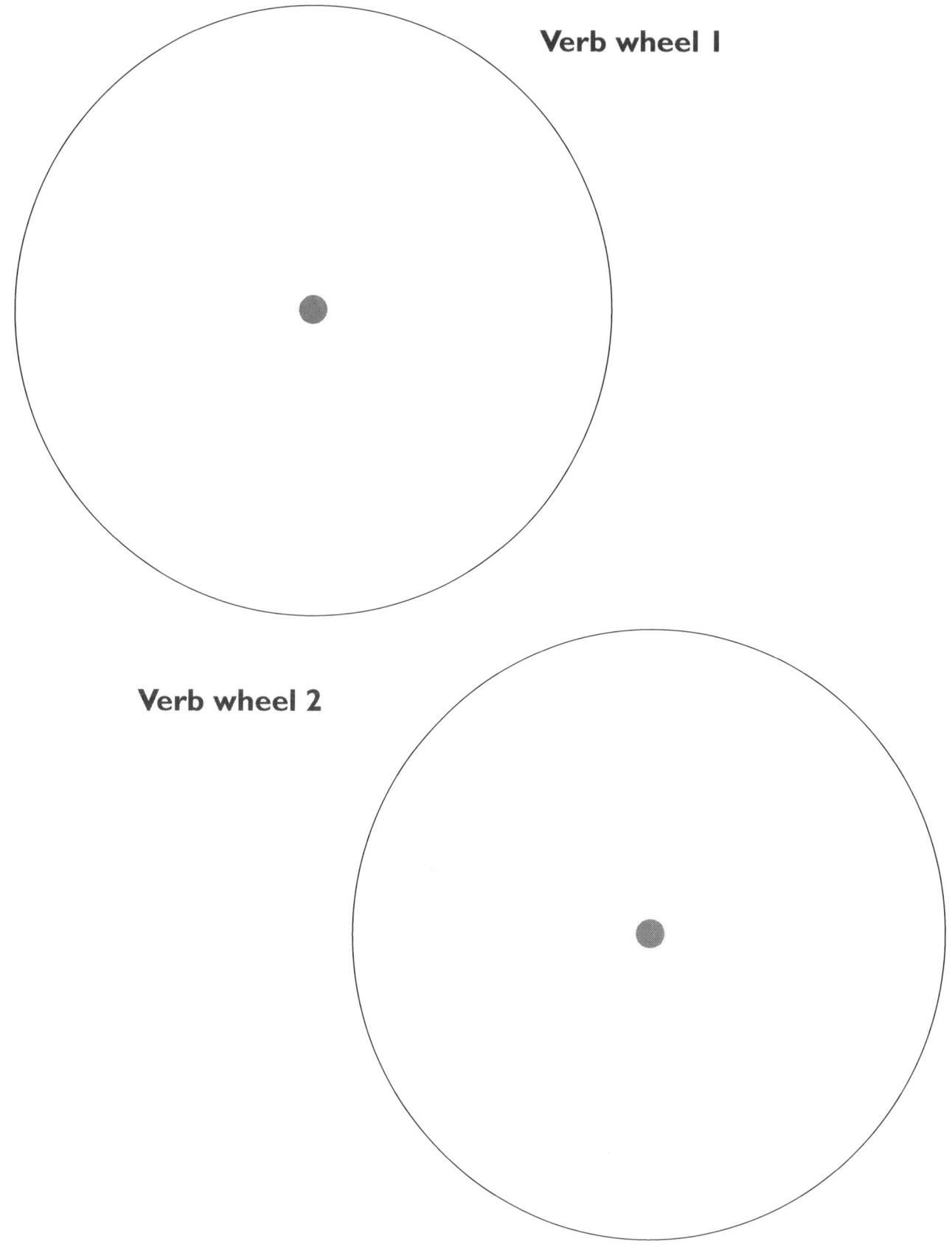

Verb wheel 1

Verb wheel 2

Irregular verbs

Learning Objectives:

- To understand that some verbs don't follow simple rules of adding 'ed' or 'd' to become past tense.

- To understand that verbs that have different spellings when describing past actions are called irregular verbs.

- To recognise and use simple common irregular verbs and their past tense.

Resources:

- **Lesson** – A display area or board, 'Word wall base verbs' and 'Past tense irregular verbs.'- (Lesson resources- CD-ROM). Sticking product such as velcro, pins to hold word wall cards to display area.

- **Group 1** – Activity sheets 1 and 2 'Irregular verb pairs'. Board or table to display a word wall.

- **Group 2** – Activity sheets 1 and 2 'Irregular verb pairs'. Small or large whiteboard and pen.

- **Group 3** - Activity sheet 3, 'Irregular verb wall'. Word bank, Word wall design ideas. (Teacher resources-CD-ROM)

Lesson/activity notes

- **Lesson** - Choose an area to create a word wall to display the pairs of irregular verbs. Create the 'Word wall base verbs' and Past tense irregular verb cards and make sure they are mixed up and on display for all the children to see. Leave a slight gap between the pair cards on the word wall so the children don't confuse the different pairs of verbs. Wall should be three pairs along and four pairs high.

- **Group 1** – Children work as a discussion group with adult support. Colour code the pairs of cards for children who have reading difficulties.

- **Group 2** – Children work as a discussion group with adult support and then two small groups.

- **Group 3** – Children work individually on the activity sheet and then in twos or threes.

Lesson

Introduction

Remind the children that verbs show what something or someone does. Remind the children how some verbs can have 'ed' to show past actions. Highlight to the children that not all verbs follow these simple rules. Some verbs change their letters in the middle, some don't change at all and some have a totally different word,

e.g. write on the board - *'I can see the sky.'* The verb 'see' doesn't become 'seed' for a past action. We use the word 'saw'. 'I saw the sky.'

Main lesson

Explain to the children that these types of verbs are called irregular verbs. Tell children that they are going to help you make a word wall using pairs of irregular verbs. Hold up the first base verb card and ask the children to read it out, e.g. see. Ask the children how they would say that verb for a past event. E.g. We saw a fish. Ask the children to see if they can find the verb card 'saw' on the display. If the children need support, read out the verbs and ask them to stop you when you say 'saw'. Put the 'see' and 'saw' cards at the bottom of the wall. Carry on with the activity until you have the word wall.

Explain to the children that they are going to do more activities with irregular verbs. Put the children into their levelled groups and give out the activities. Spend time moving between the groups to discuss individual children's work and assess their level of understanding.

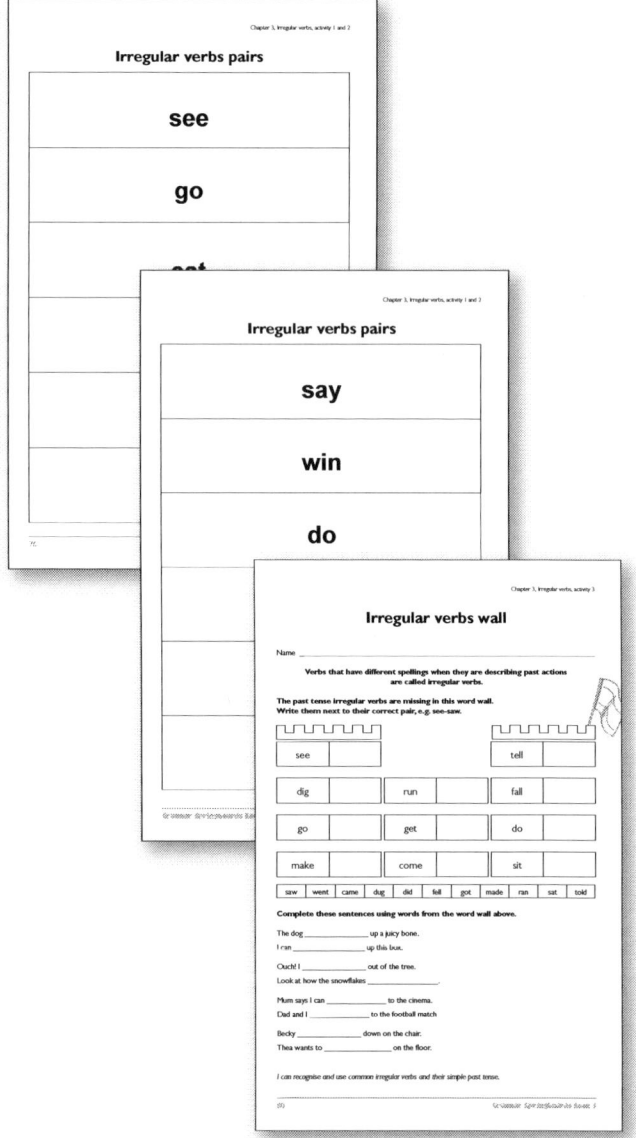

Activities

Group 1

- Show the children one pair of base and past tense verb cards such as see/saw and say two sentences using them.

- Spread out the past tense verb cards on a table or floor.

- Give each child one or two of the base verb cards and ask them to find either its matching colour card or a verb that would describe the same action in the past.

- When the pairs have been found, explain that they are going to make a castle word wall using their pairs of irregular verbs.

- Ask each child in turn to display their pairs and with the group, make simple sentences using them.

- Once the castle word wall is made, use it to help reinforce the words e.g. *Can you find me the verb, 'sat'? How is it different from 'sit'?*

Group 2:

- Show the children one pair of base and past tense verb cards such as see/saw and say two sentences using them.

- Mix up the cards and ask the children in turn to find a verb and its past tense pair.

- Go round the children in turn until all the pairs are found.

- Look at each pair and with the children and make sentences using them by writing them on a small or large white board.

- Reinforce verb recognition by playing a game of 'Pairs'. Shuffle all the cards and lay out them face down. The children take turns to turn over two cards to find the pair of verbs. They turn them back if not the right pair.

Group 3:

- Remind the children how some verbs have different spellings when they describe past actions, e.g. see/saw. Use the lesson word wall as reference.

- Give each of the children a copy of the activity sheet, 'Irregular word wall'.

- The children must add in the correct past tense verbs from a box to complete the pairs on a word wall.

- They then use some of the verbs from the word wall to complete six sentences.

- If time, encourage the children to work in twos of threes to think of some more examples of simple irregular verbs (see word bank) and create word wall shapes, e.g. bridge, tower, house.

Plenary:

Before the end of the lesson, bring all the groups together and look at the lesson word wall. Ask the children what an irregular verb is? They should say *'A verb that changes its spelling when it describes a past action.'*

Support:

Help children who need support in recognising irregular verbs by creating a little word wall of irregular verbs for their own use. They can colour code the words. In a literacy time, spend some time looking at a couple of the irregular verbs and use rhymes or pictures to reinforce them. E.g. the cat sits on the mat, the cat sat on the mat.

Extension:

Encourage the children to build up an irregular verb word bank and to use them to create poems, recounts or narratives. Ask the children if they can see any patterns in some of the irregular spellings, e.g., verbs ending with 'w' such as draw, blow, know, grow, have 'ew' at end of irregular past tense verbs - drew, blew, knew, grew.

Irregular verbs pairs

see

go

eat

come

sit

fall

Irregular verbs pairs

say
win
do
give
grow
draw

Irregular verbs pairs

saw

went

ate

came

sat

fell

Irregular verbs pairs

Grammar Springboards Book 1
said
won
did
gave
grew
drew

Irregular verbs wall

Name _____

Verbs that have different spellings when they are describing past actions are called irregular verbs.

The past tense irregular verbs are missing in this word wall.
Write them next to their correct pair, e.g. see-saw.

see	

dig		run		fall	

go		get		do	

make		come		sit	

tell	

saw	went	came	dug	did	fell	got	made	ran	sat	told

Complete these sentences using words from the word wall above.

The dog _____ up a juicy bone.

I can _____ up this box.

Ouch! I _____ out of the tree.

Look at how the snowflakes _____.

Mum says I can _____ to the cinema.

Dad and I _____ to the football match

Becky _____ down on the chair.

Thea wants to _____ on the floor.

I can recognise and use common irregular verbs and their simple past tense.

Chapter 4 – Adjectives

Adjective Information

Definition:
• Adjectives are words which describe or tell us more about a noun.

• Adjectives can make sentences more interesting.

• We can use more than one adjective together in one sentence- the tall, white mountains stood in front of them.

• Adjectives can go before a noun – e.g. *The furry cat purred.*

• Adjectives can go after a noun – e.g. *The house was very spooky.*

Types of adjective
Descriptive adjectives describe people, places, animals and objects.
E.g. The happy dragon flew into the clear sky. The round orange smelt delicious.

Number adjectives describe how many there is of a noun.
E.g. one man, two fishes, eighty doors.

Colour adjectives describe the colour of a noun.
E.g. white hair, orange face, yellow moon, red nose, blue trousers.

Shape adjectives describe the shape of a noun.
E.g. the round moon shone like a glistening diamond. The boy nervously picked up the square tin.

Grading scale of adjectives
Absolute adjectives are basic adjectives that describe a noun.
E.g. Bob has a new camera.

Comparative adjectives are adjectives that compare a noun with another.
Rule: For most comparative adjectives add –er.
E.g. Bob has got a newer camera than Millie.

Superlative adjectives are adjectives that describe a noun of the highest quality or ability.
Rule: For most superlative adjectives add –est.
E.g. Bob has got the newest camera.

Absolute	Comparative	Superlative
long	longer	longest
big	bigger	biggest
old	older	oldest

Antonyms and Synonyms Information

Antonyms

Definition:
• Antonyms are words that are the opposite meaning of another word.
  E.g. hot is the antonym of cold.

Adjective antonyms
Soft pillow/hard rock.
Bad day/good day.
Clean socks/dirty socks.

Verb antonyms
I walked to school / I ran to school
I cried / I laughed
I shouted / I whispered
I sipped my drink / I gulped my drink.
I opened the door / I closed the door.

Synonyms

Definition:
• Synonyms are words that have the same or similar meanings.
  E.g. glad, pleased, merry, thrilled are all synonyms of the word, 'happy.'

• They can be used to improve or make writing more interesting.

Synonym adjectives
angry / cross

bad -/ naughty

big / large

cold / cool

damp / wet

fat / thick

friendly / kind

Synonym verbs
Throw, toss, fling, hurl, chuck, sling.
Walk, stroll, step, ramble, hike, go, trudge.

Synonym nouns
Bush, hedge, shrub, thicket.
Pit, hole, mine, well, ditch, crater.

Adjective Springboards

Who am I?

Put the children into groups. Give them each a story character that all the children know. Ask each group to come up and use adjectives to describe the character, e.g. *'this character is young. She is very kind and helpful.'* The other children have to try and guess who it is after each descriptive sentence.

Adjective displays

With the children create pictures of different setting from a story that the children will know or could be studying as a class. Give each group a setting to draw or paint. Put the settings in order of the story and encourage the children to use adjectives to describe each one. Write adjective labels to go with the pictures.

The children could work in groups to make different story settings, e.g. a space setting, a fantasy fairy tale setting, an everyday street or school setting, a haunted house setting. Once they are displayed encourage the children to create adjective labels for their pictures.

Do the above activity with a story character or types of story characters. Encourage the children to create captions to describe the characters clothes and the characters personalities.

Give each child a picture of a person, animal, a place or an object. Give out the Word web (See teacher resources) ask the children to write down all the adjectives they can think of to describe the picture.

Ask the children to create their own story character, Let them draw a picture and use given or adjectives of their choice to write about it.

Word Walls

Create eye catching word walls. One flash card equals one brick. Have several bricks to create the word wall with the children. Have blank cards that the children can write new nouns and add to or make a new word wall shape.
They can be used in a variety of ways.

- Adjectives for different settings/ characters looks and personalities/objects

- Antonym pair

- Synonym words

The Word ladder

A similar game to 'Consequences'. In groups of four the children are given strips of paper with four sections (see Word ladder Template – Teacher resources). The children write a adjective on the first section, fold over the paper to hide it and pass it to the next child. They then write another adjective on the next and so on. After the strip has been completed it is opened up and the children read out the four written adjectives.

The children use the adjectives to describe a place, a character or an object to the rest of the children. They could also draw a picture using the adjectives.

Word wheel/ Word slide

(see Teacher resources for templates)
The teacher or children add nouns to the wheels or slides to explore and discover other words such as synonyms and antonyms. Also a good reinforcement resource.

Other ideas

- Bingo- antonyms.

- Pairs- antonyms.

- Creating and working out word searches.

- Using the star puzzle template for a quiz.

- Creating alliterative sentences using adjectives, e.g. The big bear bounced over the brown rock.

- Alphabet adjectives.

- Synonyms mobiles for a word such as snow/cold – could be icicles hanging down with the word on it, rain drops with words etc.

- Bring in an object and ask the children to use five senses to describe it, e.g., a pumpkin or orange.

Descriptive adjectives 1

Lesson

Introduction
Bring in an interesting object such as a vegetable, an unusual shaped pot. Ask children what it looks like. Write their describing words on a whiteboard. Explain that the words are called adjectives and are used to describe nouns-places, objects, people, creatures. Highlight how adjectives can make writing and reading more interesting. Give them contrasting sentences as an example, e.g. *'Kelvin picked up the teapot'* to *'Kelvin picked up the round teapot with yellow spots'*.

Main lesson
Highlight that adjectives can help readers imagine what or a place looks like. Display the children a picture, or photograph of a distinct place e.g. a snowy setting, a lush rainforest, a fantasy or a space setting. Ask the children to look closely at the scene and the objects within it e.g. mountains, trees, buildings. Encourage the children to think of adjectives to describe the nouns in the setting and write them next to the picture. By the picture, work with the children to create sentences describing the setting.

Explain to the children that they are going to do activities using adjectives to describe story settings. Put the children into their levelled groups and give out the activities. Spend time moving between the groups to discuss individual children's work and assess their level of understanding.

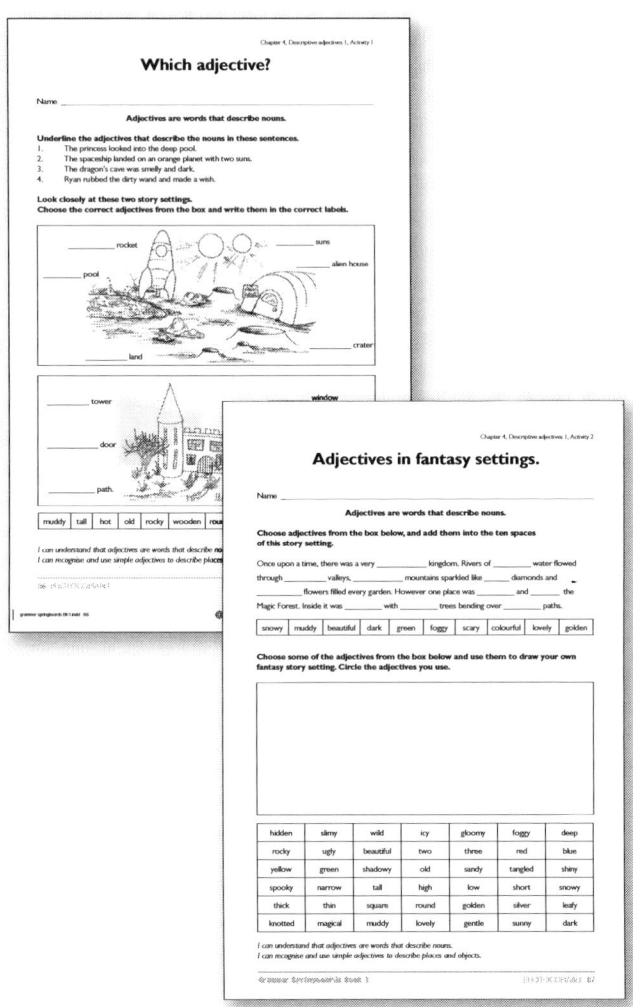

Activities

Group 1
- Give the children a choice of fantasy story settings or let them choose their own. E.g. an alien garden, a dragon's cave, a magic wood, a school or town in the future, an ogre's castle.

- Ask them to draw and colour their story setting on the blank paper.

- Once the children have completed their drawings, ask each child what adjectives they would use to describe the nouns in their setting.

- Write the adjectives down on the card or paper labels.

- Ask the rest of the children for other adjectives that could be used and write them out.

- Display their work with the adjective word labels around each setting picture.

Group 2:
- With the children as a group, discuss how adjectives can help describe imaginary worlds by looking at examples in a few stories and books.

- Give out the copies of 'Which adjective?' to the each child.

- Working individually, the children underline the adjectives in the four sentences.

- The children then match the adjectives to two story settings pictures by writing them in the correct boxes under the right pictures.

- On a separate piece of paper, the children draw their own story setting and write adjectives underneath their picture.

Group 3:
- With the children as a group, discuss how adjectives can help describe imaginary worlds by looking at examples in a few stories and books.

- Give the copies of 'Adjectives in fantasy settings' to each child.

- Working individually, the children add adjectives to complete a short passage.

- They then draw their own fantasy setting from a choice of adjectives, circling the ones they used.

- Once they have completed the drawings, ask the children to pair-share their work.

- Encourage them to think of other adjectives they could add to the picture.

Plenary:
Before the end of the lesson, bring the groups together. Discuss their setting pictures and the adjectives used to describe the nouns in the settings. Highlight that adjectives can make writing more fun and interesting and help readers imagine places and objects more clearly.

Support:
Use the senses to help children use adjectives to describe objects. Bring in fruit, vegetables or flowers and show it to the child. Ask the child to use the senses to describe the object, e.g. smell=sweet, feels=slimy, looks=red, sounds=crunchy.

Extension:
Make a pile of adjective cards and put them in a pile in front of the children. Let the children take turns to pick an adjective and then use a small whiteboard or paper to write a sentence using the picked adjective. Increase the number of adjective cards per sentence as they get more able.

Which adjective?

Name _____

Adjectives are words that describe nouns.

Underline the adjectives that describe the nouns in these sentences.
1.   The princess looked into the deep pool.
2.   The spaceship landed on an orange planet with two suns.
3.   The dragon's cave was smelly and dark.
4.   Ryan rubbed the dirty wand and made a wish.

Look closely at these two story settings.
Choose the correct adjectives from the box and write them in the correct labels.

muddy	tall	hot	old	rocky	wooden	round	high	two	spooky	wide	square

I can understand that adjectives are words that describe nouns.
I can recognise and use simple adjectives to describe places and objects.

Adjectives in fantasy settings.

Name _____

Adjectives are words that describe nouns.

Choose adjectives from the box below, and add them into the ten spaces of this story setting.

Once upon a time, there was a very _____ kingdom. Rivers of _____ water flowed

through _____ valleys, _____ mountains sparkled like _____ diamonds and

_____ flowers filled every garden. However one place was _____ and _____ the

Magic Forest. Inside it was _____ with _____ trees bending over _____ paths.

snowy	muddy	beautiful	dark	green	foggy	scary	colourful	lovely	golden

Choose some of the adjectives from the box below and use them to draw your own fantasy story setting. Circle the adjectives you use.

hidden	slimy	wild	icy	gloomy	foggy	deep
rocky	ugly	beautiful	two	three	red	blue
yellow	green	shadowy	old	sandy	tangled	shiny
spooky	narrow	tall	high	low	short	snowy
thick	thin	square	round	golden	silver	leafy
knotted	magical	muddy	lovely	gentle	sunny	dark

I can understand that adjectives are words that describe nouns.
I can recognise and use simple adjectives to describe places and objects.

Descriptive adjectives 2

- To understand that adjectives are words that tell us more about nouns.

- To understand that adjectives can help you imagine what someone looks like.

- To recognise and use simple adjectives to describe people or creatures.

Resources:
- **Lesson** –Story character picture – (Lesson resources-CD ROM) Pictures or photos of a variety of creatures, e.g. animals, birds, mini-beasts, reptiles, sea-life.

- **Group 1** – Copies of activity sheet 1, 'Story characters', and activity sheet 1.2 'My story character' for each child. Scissors, glue, pencils, colouring pencils.

- **Group 2** – Copies of activity sheet 2, 'Wanted!' for each child. Pencils, colouring pencils, Copies of 'Adjectives consequences'- (Lesson resources-CD ROM).

- **Group 3** – Copies of activity sheet 3 'Describing a story character'. Pencils, colouring pencils, Copies of 'Adjectives of characters' consequences'- (Lesson resources-CD ROM).

Lesson/activity notes
- **Group 1** – Children work individually on their activity sheet with adult support.

- **Group 2** – Children work individually on their activity sheet and as a group playing, 'Adjective consequences.'

- **Group 3** – Children work individually on their activity sheet and as a group playing, 'Adjective consequences.

Lesson

Introduction
Show the picture of the story character to the children. Ask the children to think of words to describe the character. Write the words around the character. Highlight that these words are called adjectives. Highlight how adjectives can make story characters more interesting or describe their special features.

Main lesson
Explain that adjectives can give a lot of information. They can be numbers, colour, size, shape, moods. Draw a table on the white board with subtitles - (**Colour, Number, Size, Shape, Touch**). Put the children into groups of two or three and give each group a photograph or picture of creature to study, e.g. elephant, cat,

parrot, octopus, spider, snake. In turn ask each group to give you adjectives for each heading to describe their creature and write them in the table, e.g. one trunk, wrinkly skin, slimy skin. Underline the adjectives.

Explain to the children that they are going to work in groups to do activities using adjectives to describe story characters. Put the children into their levelled groups and give out the activities. Spend time moving between the groups to discuss individual children's work and assess their level of understanding.

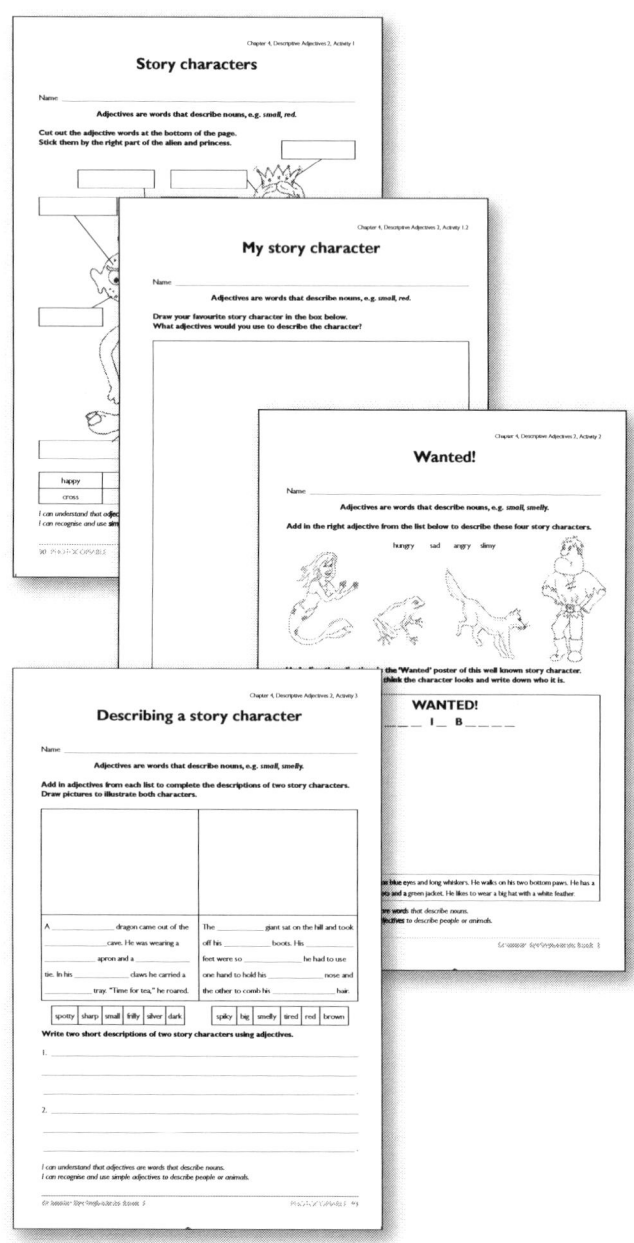

Activities

Group 1
- Give the children copies of activity sheet 1 'Story characters' to each of the children.

- Working individually, the children cut out the adjective labels.

Grammar Springboards Book 1

- With adult support, the children read the adjective labels and stick them by the right character.

- When they have completed the characters, ask them to describe each one using the adjectives in sentences, e.g. *The prince has a long sword.*

- If time, give each of the children copies of activity sheet 1.2, 'My story character'.

- Ask them to draw their favourite story character and encourage them to think of the adjectives to describe the character.

- Write down their adjectives for them to use as labels or help them write out the words.

Group 2

- Give copies of activity sheet 2, 'Wanted!' to each child.

- Working individually, the children add in the right adjective from a given list to describe four story characters.

- The children then underline the adjectives of a description of well known story character on 'Wanted' poster.

- The children can then draw a picture of the character and add the character's name on the poster –Puss in Boots.

- Discuss with the children how the adjectives give the reader a clearer picture of the character.

Group 3:

- Give the children copies of the activity sheet 3, 'Describing a story character,'

- Working individually, the children add in adjectives from a list to describe two story characters and then draw pictures to illustrate the characters.

- Then they write two short descriptions to describe two of their own story characters.

- Encourage the children to share their descriptions and discuss how adjectives can give a clearer picture of a character.

Plenary:

Before the end of the lesson, bring the groups together. Ask the children about the characters that they have created or described in their activities. Remind the children how adjectives can make their writing more fun and interesting and help readers imagine story characters more clearly.

Support:

Use drama and role play to help children use adjectives. Put them on a hot-seat and ask them to describe a fellow character and their personality. Look at good and bad characters. Write down the adjectives so that they can be used as a word bank for the children.

Extension:

Encourage the children to look at a variety of fictional, non-fictional and poetry texts for examples of adjectives that describe people and creatures. Suggest they create a word bank to collect adjective examples.

Story characters

Name _____

Adjectives are words that describe nouns, e.g. *small, red.*

Cut out the adjective words at the bottom of the page.
Stick them by the right part of the alien and princess.

happy	spotty	long	flowery	slimy
cross	one	big	small	two

I can understand that adjectives are words that describe nouns.
I can recognise and use simple adjectives to describe people or animals.

My story character

Name _____

Adjectives are words that describe nouns, e.g. *small, red*.

**Draw your favourite story character in the box below.
What adjectives would you use to describe the character?**

I can understand that adjectives are words that describe nouns.
I can recognise and use simple adjectives to describe people or animals.

Wanted!

Name _____

Adjectives are words that describe nouns, e.g. *small, smelly.*

Add in the right adjective from the list below to describe these four story characters.

hungry   sad   angry   slimy

Underline the adjectives in the 'Wanted' poster of this well known story character. Draw a picture of how you think the character looks and write down who it is.

WANTED!
P _ _ _   I _   B _ _ _ _

He is a black and white cat. He has blue eyes and long whiskers. He walks on his two bottom paws. He has a cheeky smile. He wears large boots and a green jacket. He likes to wear a big hat with a white feather.

I can understand that adjectives are words that describe nouns.
I can recognise and use simple adjectives to describe people or animals.

Describing a story character

Name _____

Adjectives are words that describe nouns, e.g. *small, smelly*.

Add in adjectives from each list to complete the descriptions of two story characters. Draw pictures to illustrate both characters.

A _____ dragon came out of the _____ cave. He was wearing a _____ apron and a _____ tie. In his _____ claws he carried a _____ tray. "Time for tea," he roared.

The _____ giant sat on the hill and took off his _____ boots. His _____ feet were so _____ he had to use one hand to hold his _____ nose and the other to comb his _____ hair.

spotty	sharp	small	frilly	silver	dark

spiky	big	smelly	tired	red	brown

Write two short descriptions of two story characters using adjectives.

1. _____

_____

_____ .

2. _____

_____

_____ .

I can understand that adjectives are words that describe nouns.
I can recognise and use simple adjectives to describe people or animals.

Opposites - Antonyms

Learning Objectives:
- To understand that an antonym word is the opposite meaning of another word.

- To recognise and use antonyms as adjectives.

Resources:
- **Lesson:** 'Word Bank' adjective antonym examples.

- **Group 1** – A set of activity sheet 1 'Opposite pairs cards' for each pair of children and two blank cards or paper per child.

- **Group 2** – Copies of activity sheet 2, 'An Opposite Poem,' for each child.

- **Group 3** – Copies of activity sheet, 'An Antonym Poem' for each child.

Lesson/activity notes
- **Group 1** – Copy and cut out the activity sheet 1, 'Opposite pairs cards' for each pair of children. The children work as pairs and then individually to create new antonyms. The group will need adult support.

- **Group 2** – Children work individually on the activity sheet. They share their poems with the group.

- **Group 3** – Children work individually on the activity sheet. They pair-share their poems.

Lesson

Introduction
Explain to the children that they are going to find out about antonyms. Highlight that an antonym word is the opposite of another word. Explain that they are going to look at the opposites of different adjectives. Give an example, 'The opposite of the adjective 'happy' is 'sad'.' Play a game where you say an adjective to a pair of children and they say the opposite, e.g. fat / thin. Do this with all the children and write them on the board.

Main lesson
Explain to the children that as a class they are going to create a nonsense poem using the opposites recorded on the board. Start off the nonsense poem by doing the first two lines e.g. When I'm small, I feel big.' Encourage the children to continue the poem in the same pattern by contributing more adjective antonyms. Once the poem has been written, read it out with the class. After the lesson, copy out the poem and display it for the class to see. They could each have a copy to illustrate and keep.

Explain to the children that they are going to work in groups to do activities on antonyms. Put the children into their levelled

groups and give out the activities. Spend time moving between the groups to discuss individual children's work and assess their level of understanding.

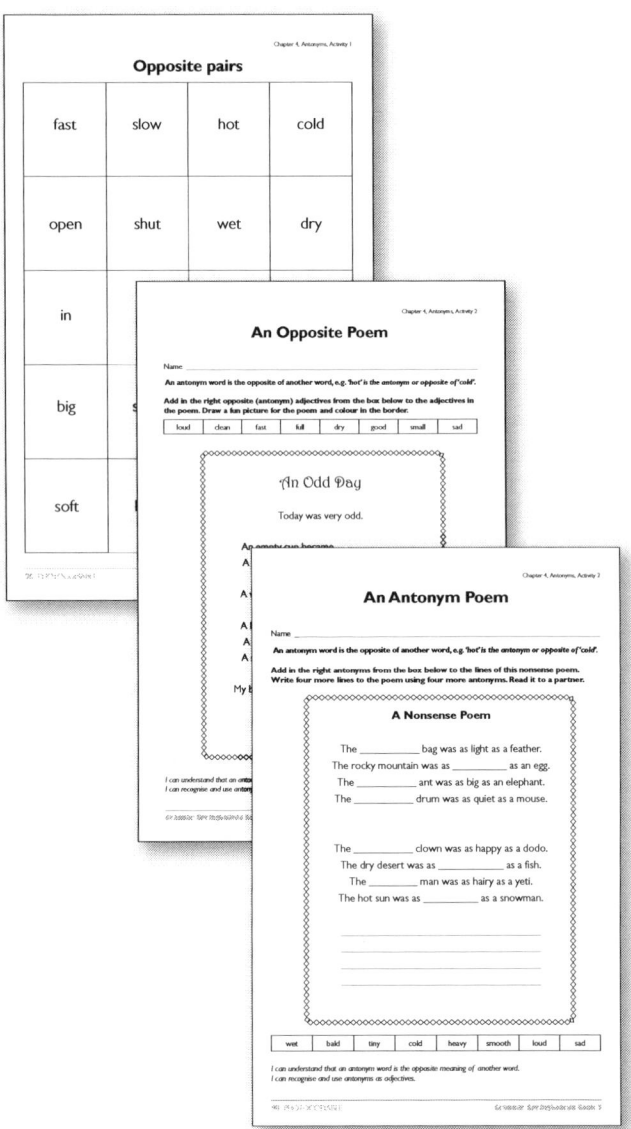

Activities

Group 1
- Put the children into pairs and ask them to lay out a set of shuffled 'Opposite pair cards' face down in front of them.

- The children take turns to turn over two cards to find an opposite pair, e.g. hot / cold.

- If they find a pair they take the two cards. If they don't, they turn the cards back over.

- Once the two children have got all the pairs, discuss the different opposites.

- Give each child two blank cards and ask them to think of another pair of opposites.

- They then draw pictures on each card to illustrate their opposites.

- Let them show their cards to their partner and help them write the words underneath.

Group 2:
- Give out the activity sheet 2, 'An Opposite Poem' to each child.

- Working individually, the children complete a poem by choosing the right antonym from a list to match the adjective in each line of the poem.

- They then draw a picture at the end of the poem and colour the border.

- At the end of the activity, discuss with children their adjective opposites and the fun effect on the poem.

- If time, ask the children to think of four more opposites to add to the poem.

Group 3:
- Give out the activity sheet 3, 'An Antonym Poem' to each child.

- Working individually, the children complete a poem frame by choosing adjective antonyms from a list.

- Finally they write four more lines in their own words and choice of adjective antonyms.

- The children share their poems with a partner and discuss the antonyms used.

Plenary:
Before the end of the lesson, bring all the groups together. Discuss the adjective opposites each group used in their activities. Ask the children what name we call words that are opposites of other words-antonyms. Highlight that antonyms are used quite a bit in stories, e.g. good vs. bad characters, big giant vs. little person.

Support:
For children who need support, play various games such as matching opposite pictures on a bingo style board, role playing different characteristics e.g. loud/quiet, good/bad. Build word walls of antonyms using cards with words and pictures. These could be made by the children.

Extension:
Encourage the children to list or find more adjective antonyms. Encourage them to use some of the antonyms to create two opposite story character profiles using pictures and captions.

Opposite pairs

fast	slow	hot	cold
open	shut	wet	dry
in	out	full	empty
big	small	dirty	clean
soft	hard	loud	quiet

An Opposite Poem

Name _____

An antonym word is the opposite of another word, e.g. 'hot' is the antonym or opposite of 'cold'.

Add in the right opposite (antonym) adjectives from the box below to the adjectives in the poem. Draw a fun picture for the poem and colour in the border.

loud	clean	fast	full	dry	good	small	sad

An Odd Day

Today was very odd.

An empty cup became _____,
A happy clown became _____,
A dirty sock became _____,
A wet bath became _____.

A big giant became _____
A quiet mouse became _____,
A slow snail became _____,
And
My bad sister became _____!

Yes, today was very odd.

I can understand that an antonym word is the opposite meaning of another word.
I can recognise and use antonyms as adjectives.

An Antonym Poem

Name _____

An antonym word is the opposite of another word, e.g. 'hot' is the antonym or opposite of 'cold'.

Add in the right antonyms from the box below to the lines of this nonsense poem.
Write four more lines to the poem using four more antonyms. Read it to a partner.

A Nonsense Poem

The _____ bag was as light as a feather.

The rocky mountain was as _____ as an egg.

The _____ ant was as big as an elephant.

The _____ drum was as quiet as a mouse.

The _____ clown was as happy as a dodo.

The dry desert was as _____ as a fish.

The _____ man was as hairy as a yeti.

The hot sun was as _____ as a snowman.

_____

_____

_____

_____

wet	bald	tiny	cold	heavy	smooth	loud	sad

I can understand that an antonym word is the opposite meaning of another word.
I can recognise and use antonyms as adjectives.

Synonyms - adjectives

Learning Objectives

- To understand that synonyms are words that have the same or similar meaning e.g. big, large.

- To understand how synonyms can make writing more interesting.

- To recognise and use synonyms as adjectives.

Resources:

- **Lesson** – Picture of a mouse. Picture of an elephant, 'The great day'- (Teacher resources-CD-ROM)

- **Group 1** – Copy and cut out the pictures from activity sheets 1.1 and 1.2 'Hot or Cold?' Stick each picture onto a large piece of paper or sugar paper with room around the sides to write synonyms, pen.

- **Group 2** – Copies of activity sheet 2, 'Happy or Sad?' for each child, blank paper.

- **Group 3** – Copies of activity sheet 3, 'Amazing animals' for each child.

Lesson/activity notes

- **Group 1** – Children work in a discussion group with the adult/teacher acting as a scribe. The activity can also be used in smaller groups or one to one if required.

- **Group 2** – Children work individually on the activity sheet and then in pairs.

- **Group 3** – Children work individually on the activity sheet and discuss results with a teacher.

Lesson

Introduction

Show the picture of the mouse to the children. Ask the children what the word is on the cheese -'small'. Ask the children to think of other words that mean the same or are similar as 'small' such as 'tiny'. Write each word around the mouse. Explain that words that have the same or similar meaning are called synonyms. Highlight that the synonym words used in the mouse picture are all adjectives.

Main lesson

Explain how a synonym can make writing a lot more interesting. Show 'The Great Day' and read it out. Discuss how the text is quite boring as the word 'great' is used all the time. With the children write down as many synonyms as they can for the word 'great' Ask various children to choose one of the synonyms to replace 'great' words in the text. Read it out and discuss how it has made the writing more interesting.

Explain to the children that they are going to work in groups to do activities on synonyms. Put the children into their levelled groups and give out the activities. Spend time moving between the groups to discuss individual children's work and assess their level of understanding.

Activities

Group 1

- Show one of the pictures to the children, e.g. the snow picture.

- Ask the children what they would feel if they were standing in the picture.

- Write the word, 'cold' by the picture and ask the children to think of other words that could also describe 'cold'.

- Write down their ideas. Ask open ended questions or give clues of words if some children need support.

- Do the same with the hot landscape picture.

- At the end, read through the words on each picture.

- Highlight that words which have the same or similar meanings are called synonyms.

Group 2

- Give out the activity sheet 2 'Happy or Sad?' to each child.

- Working individually, the children cut up labels of synonyms and match them to the happy clown and sad clown faces.

- They are then asked to add in two more synonyms to each face.

- The children are then asked to add their choice of synonyms to four sentences.

- If there is time, ask the children to draw an angry face and in pairs think and record synonyms for 'angry'.

Group 3

- Give out the activity sheet 3, 'Amazing animals' to each child.

- Working individually, the children choose the right synonyms to replace words in sentences.

- They then add in synonyms next to words to complete a passage about a polar bear.

- Finally they draw a polar bear with labels taken from the passage.

- Once the children have completed the sheet, ask them how synonyms can change a piece of writing, e.g. the polar bear passage.

Plenary:

Before the end of the lesson, bring all the groups together. Ask each group for examples of synonyms from their activities. Ask the children what a synonym is. Call out an adjective such as brave and ask the class or a group to tell you a synonym. Do a few more to consolidate their knowledge.

Support

Help support those who need more support by bringing in objects, or show pictures e.g. a giant or an apple. Choose one word such as tall, smooth and ask the children to think of similar words. Write them on labels and make a display or a mobile.

Extension:

Explain to the children that synonyms can also be found in nouns and verbs. Show the children a simple thesaurus and encourage them to choose two words and make word web displays of their synonyms. (Word web- Teacher resources)

Hot or Cold?

Hot or Cold?

Happy or Sad?

Name _____

Synonyms are words that have the same or similar meaning, e.g. *big, large*.

**Cut out the synonym labels below and stick them by the sad or happy clown.
Add two more 'happy' and 'sad' synonyms to each clown.**

Complete the sentences below using four of the synonyms.

1.   The _____ clown told a joke and made everyone laugh.

2.   The _____ clown didn't want to be funny.

3.   The _____ clown laughed and sang all day.

4.   The _____ clown missed his mum and dad.

happy	glum	merry	sad
cheerful	unhappy	gloomy	jolly

*I understand that synonyms are words that have the same meaning or similar meaning.
I can recognise and use synonyms as adjectives.*

Amazing animals

Name _____

Synonyms are words that have the same or similar meaning, e.g. *big, large*.

Choose the right synonym from the box to replace the underlined words in the sentences.

wet	pointed	tall	quick	larger	powerful

1.   Frogs have <u>strong</u> legs to help them leap.   _____

2.   A grizzly bear can run as <u>fast</u> as a horse.   _____

3.   A giraffe uses its <u>long</u> neck to reach leaves. _____

4.   An ostrich eye is <u>bigger</u> than its brain. _____

5.   The toucan uses its <u>sharp</u> bill to crack nuts. _____

6.   Beetles like to live in <u>damp</u> earth. _____

Choose synonyms from the list below and write them next to the right adjectives in this information about a polar bear.

chunky   bumpy   icy   quietly   biggest

Polar bears

Polar bears live in very cold (_____) places. They are the largest (_____)

bears in the world. Their thick (_____), white fur keeps them warm. They have rough

(_____) paw pads to stop them slipping on the ice. They hunt seals by waiting

silently (_____) by a seal hole and then jumping on them.

Draw a picture of a polar bear in the box below and label using the information from above, e.g. thick, white fur.

I understand that synonyms are words that have the same meaning or similar meaning.
I can recognise and use synonyms as adjectives.

Chapter 5 – Making sentences

Sentence information

Sentences
- Subject of a sentence – what or who the sentence is about
- Predicate of a sentence – part of the sentence that does not include the subject e.g. the verb.

Clause -
- Main clause – Main part of a sentence. *E.g. I'll make you a cup of tea, after this.*
- Subordinate - It give more information about the main clause in a sentence,
  E.g. Harry felt sick, when he got home.

Simple sentences
A simple sentence is made up of a subject and a predicate *E.g. Julia (subject) fell off the see-saw. (Predicate).*
Sentences begin with a capital letter and finish with a full stop, question mark or an exclamation mark.

Capital letters
Capital letters used for a number of reasons:
1. At the beginning of a sentence e.g. *'Today we are going for a walk'*.
2. For proper nouns, e.g. *Mary, Rose Road, The Three Bears*.
3. To emphasise certain words in a phrase or sentence, e.g. *'Watch OUT!'*

Compound sentences
A compound sentence is made from two simple sentences joined together by a conjunction.

Connectives
Connectives are words or phrases that join different parts of a text.
There are several types of connectives:
1. conjunctions.
2. prepositions.
3. adverbs
4. pronouns (see pronoun information)

Conjunctions
Conjunctions links words and sentences using and, but, or, so, if, yet.
E.g. *I like soup <u>and</u> I like bread.*
  Joe likes oranges <u>but</u> he doesn't like orange juice.
  Do you want chips <u>or</u> do you want rice?
  I have a cold <u>so</u> I am in bed.

Time connectives
Time connectives are words and phrases used in sentences to highlight the chronological time of the main subject – first, then , next, later, tomorrow, just then, afterwards.
E.g. *I will do my homework in a <u>minute</u>. <u>First</u> I must have a biscuit.*

Prepositions

Prepositions are connective words that describe where someone or something is within a sentence, e.g. under, above, on, behind, below. A preposition is usually before the noun.
E.g. *The man sat <u>on</u> the bench. I put the duvet <u>over</u> my head.*

Sentence springboards

Word Walls

Create eye catching word walls. One flash card equals one brick. Have several bricks to create the word wall with the children. Have blank cards that the children can write new words and add to or make a new word wall shape. Use a Word wall for the children to create simple sentences. Create challenges by mixing up words in sentences and asking the children to put them into the right order.

The Word ladder

A similar game to 'Consequences'.
In groups of four the children are given strips of paper with four sections (see Word ladder Template – Teacher resources). The children write a short sentence on the first section, fold over the paper to hide it and pass it to the next child. They then write another short sentence in the next and so on. After the strip has been completed it is opened up and the children read out the four written sentences.
The game can be used in a variety of ways:

- Simple sentences; Use the simple sentences to create a fun, nonsense story or poem.

- Compound sentences: Ask the children to use 'but' between each sentence or they could also choose 'so' 'or'.

- Time connectives. The children choose a character and then use time connectives orally to recount what the character did, e.g. First she went to the moon, then she swam with mermaids etc.

Short sentences

Give a group or pair of children a five or six letter word, e.g. robot. Ask the children to write the letters going down the page. They then have to make up a simple sentence messages using the letters as the first words of each sentence, e.g. *Red apples are very tasty. Owls come out at night. Bob loves to eat pizza. Oranges make great drinks. The balloon flew away.*

Instruction book

Have a 'How to do it' book made by the class. They all contribute how to make or cook something. Set out a frame that they could all use and highlight the use of time connectives. Encourage the children to draw diagrams to go with their instructions.

Find the letters

Ask the children to follow the clues which use prepositions to find letters that create a word. Let the children make up their own treasure hunts or hunt the letters with clues using prepositions.

Other activities

- Explore tongue twisters and fun poetry and rhymes.

- I-spy using prepositions.

- Fun t-shirt or captions for a bag or badge.

- Create short sentences for posters

- Flip book sentences use card and rings. Add several word cards on each ring. Have words with capital letters on the first ring and words with full stops on the last ring. Children can have fun flipping over the words to make sentences.

- Look at a local map or map of the school and place pin or sticker on one place. Ask the children to use prepositions to show directions to the place.

- Kim's game. Look at a picture before it is taken away and then use prepositions to explain where objects or people are

- Cut out sentences in a weekly comic. Ask children to match them to the pictures in right order.

- The good and bad news game: -The children use conjunctions to say a piece of good news followed by a funny piece of bad news about story characters. E.g. *The good news is that Big Billy Goat Gruff has got rid of the troll but the bad news is all the grass has been eaten by the other goats.*

Simple Sentences

Lesson

Introduction
Show the picture 'A Celtic hut' to the children and explain that it was a home people lived in many years ago in Britain during Roman times. With the children read out the labels. Highlight how the labels are only one or two words. Explain that you are going to use one of the labels to write a simple sentence about the Celtic hut, e.g. *The hut has mud walls*. Highlight that a sentence is a group of words that makes sense. Use different highlighters to underline the different features of the sentence, e.g. capital letter to start, the main subject and a full stop.

Main lesson
Explain that you would like to create an information display of homes through the ages and need simple sentences to go with each home. Display one house picture at a time to the children.

Ask the children to think of one simple sentence about the house. Write the sentences on the board, with open ended prompts about using capital letters and full stops. Once all the sentences are written on the board, read through them with the class. Highlight the beginning and end of each sentence and the punctuation. Do the same with the other houses. At a later point, create the display with the children's simple sentences.

Explain to the children that they are going to work on activities on simple sentences.

Put the children into their levelled groups and give out the activities. Spend time moving between the groups to discuss individual children's work and assess their level of understanding.

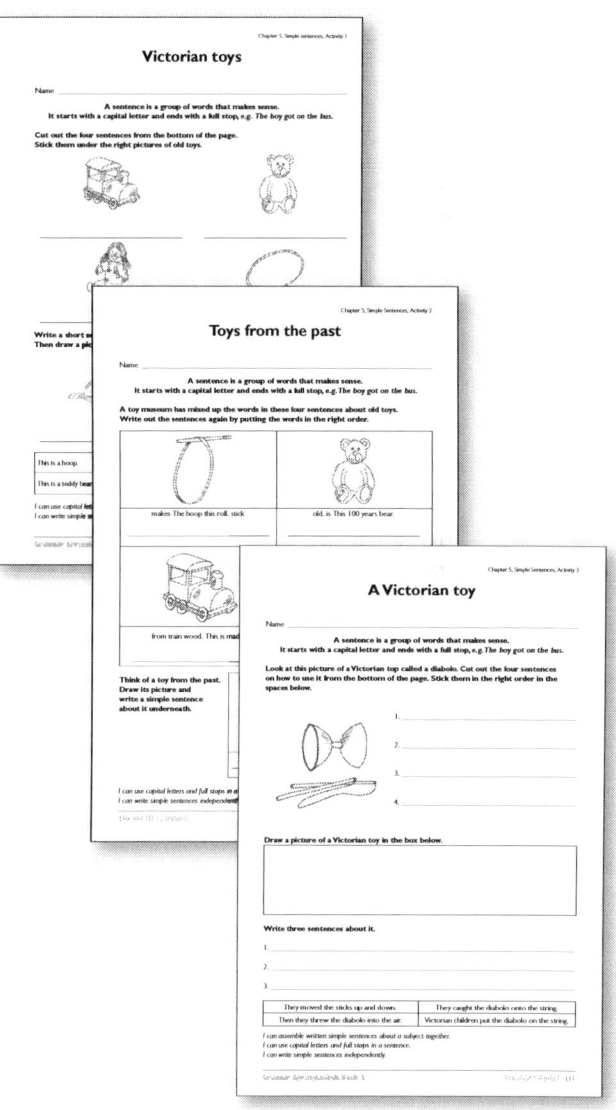

Activities

Group 1
- Give out the copies of 'Victorian toys' to each child.

- As a group, look at the first four pictures of Victorian toys and read the sentences at the bottom of the page.

- The children cut out the sentences and stick them under the matching toy.

- Ask the children to underline the capital letter and full stop in each sentence.

- Let them write a simple sentence in the same sentence pattern and draw a picture to go with it.

Group 2:
- Give out the copies of 'Toys from the past', to each child.

- The children must rewrite the mixed up words of four sentences about old toys.

- Ask which two rules for writing sentences give clues to the first and last words in the sentences – capital letter and full stop.

- The children then draw a picture of an old toy with a simple sentence underneath it.

- At the end of the activity discuss how simple sentences in museum displays are called captions.

Group 3:
- Give out the copies of 'A Victorian toy' to each child.

- Working individually, the children look at a picture of a Victorian Diabolo.

- The children cut out the sentences then reassemble and stick them into a coherent group of sentences about how a Diablo was used.

- Discuss how the order of the sentences must make sense.

- The children then draw a picture of a Victorian toy of their own choice followed by three sentences about it.

Plenary:
Before the end of the lesson, bring the groups together. Ask the children to give examples of their simple sentences about a Victorian toy. Write the sentences on the board. Ask the children what they need to remember when writing a sentence. Highlight the features as they are given, e.g. capital letter, full stop.

Support:
For children who need more support, create simple sentence chains with a word per chain, e.g. The man had a car. The more words there are the more sentences they could create. Design ideas could include a sentence train with carriages, caterpillar etc.

Extension:
Encourage the children to create a fact file on a non-fiction subject using simple sentences for each fact. Discuss the order in which the information and sentences can be ordered.

Victorian toys

Name _____

**A sentence is a group of words that makes sense.
It starts with a capital letter and ends with a full stop, e.g. *The boy got on the bus.***

**Cut out the four sentences from the bottom of the page.
Stick them under the right pictures of old toys.**

**Write a short sentence for the picture below.
Then draw a picture for the last toy.**

_____   This is a rocking horse

This is a hoop.	This is a doll.
This is a teddy bear.	This is a train.

I can use capital letters and full stops in a sentence.
I can write simple sentences independently.

Toys from the past

Name _____

A sentence is a group of words that makes sense.
It starts with a capital letter and ends with a full stop, e.g. *The boy got on the bus.*

A toy museum has mixed up the words in these four sentences about old toys.
Write out the sentences again by putting the words in the right order.

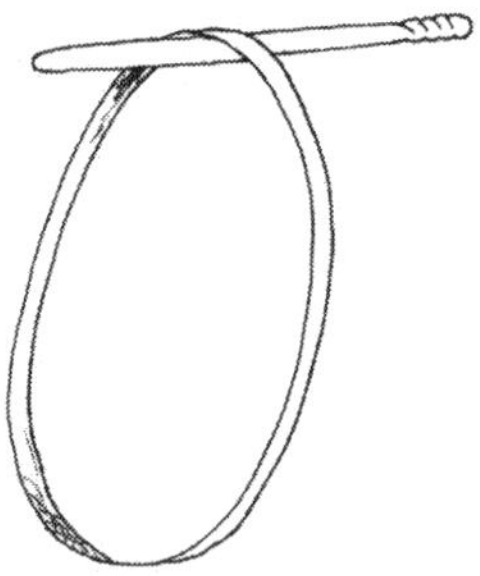 makes The hoop this roll. stick	 old. is This 100 years bear.
 _____	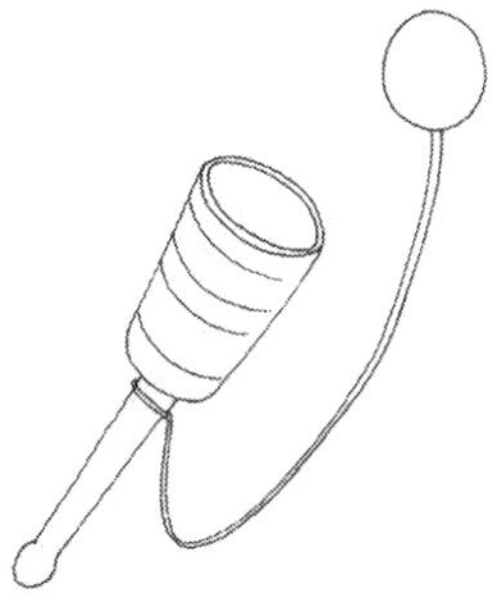 _____
from train wood. This is made	swung ball The into cup. Wooden is the
_____	_____

Think of a toy from the past.
Draw its picture and
write a simple sentence
about it underneath.

_____

I can use capital letters and full stops in a sentence.
I can write simple sentences independently.

A Victorian toy

Name _____

**A sentence is a group of words that makes sense.
It starts with a capital letter and ends with a full stop, e.g. *The boy got on the bus.***

Look at this picture of a Victorian top called a diabolo. Cut out the four sentences on how to use it from the bottom of the page. Stick them in the right order in the spaces below.

1. _____

2. _____

3. _____

4. _____

Draw a picture of a Victorian toy in the box below.

Write three sentences about it.

1. _____

2. _____

3. _____

They moved the sticks up and down.	They caught the diabolo onto the string.
Then they threw the diabolo into the air.	Victorian children put the diabolo on the string.

I can assemble written simple sentences about a subject together.
I can use capital letters and full stops in a sentence.
I can write simple sentences independently.

Compound Sentences

Learning Objectives:
- To understand that two simple sentences joined into a long sentence is called a compound sentence.

- To understand that joining words (conjunctions) such as 'and', 'but' 'so' and 'or' can create compound sentences.

- To recognise the effect in a text by using compound sentences.

Resources:
- **Lesson** – 'The sticky lollipop', 'Sticky lollipop short sentences', 'Joining words flash cards' (Lesson Resources – CD-ROM).

- **Group 1** – One copy of activity sheet 1.1, 'Compound sentences' for the group. Whiteboard or computer. Mini books (see notes below), colouring pencils.

- **Group 2** — Copies of activity sheet 2, 'Making compound sentences' for each child. Mini books (see notes below), colouring pencils.

- **Group 3** - Copies of activity sheet 3, 'Compound sentence story' for each child. Mini books (see notes below), colouring pencils.

Lesson/activity notes
- **Lesson** – In this lesson we have used 'Joining words' instead of the term 'conjunctions.' Choose which term is suitable for the skills and understanding of the children.

- **Mini Books** – Zig zag book instructions' and 'Slit book instructions' (Teacher resources-CD-ROM). The Zig Zag or Slit mini books can be made in advance depending on timing of lesson and skills of children. Use A3 card or paper if possible. Children could use the computer to write and then print out their sentences for their books.

- **Group 1** – Children work as a discussion group with teacher/adult support as scribe. Cut out the sentences and joining words from the activity sheet before the lesson. Be near a whiteboard or a computer for writing out compound sentences. The children work individually on their mini-books.

- **Group 2** – Children work in pairs on their activity sheets. They work individually on writing their mini books and then share their work. Teacher discussion needed when activity sheet is completed.

- **Group 3** – Children work individually on the activity sheet and their compound story book. They pair-share their books at the end of the activity.

Lesson

Introduction
Read the story 'The sticky lollipop' to the children. Show or copy 'Sticky lollipop short sentences' onto a whiteboard. Highlight that we can make one long sentence by joining two of the short sentences together. Explain that these long sentences are called compound sentences. Introduce and display the three 'Joining words flash cards 'and', 'but' and 'or'. Explain that these words are used to join two short sentences into one compound sentence.

Main lesson
Suggest to the children that they help you join the 'Sticky lollipop short sentences' into compound sentences by using the joining words 'and', 'but' and 'or'. Model the first two short sentences by adding 'and'. Note how the full stop of the first sentence and the beginning capital letter are not used. Discuss the improved effect of the sentence. With the children, change the rest of the sentences. Encourage children to come up and put the joining word card between the sentences. Read through the resulting compound sentences and highlight how compound sentences can make their writing flow and be more interesting.

Explain to the children that they are going to do activities on compound sentences. Put the children into their levelled groups and give out the activities. Spend time moving between the groups to discuss individual children's work and assess their level of understanding.

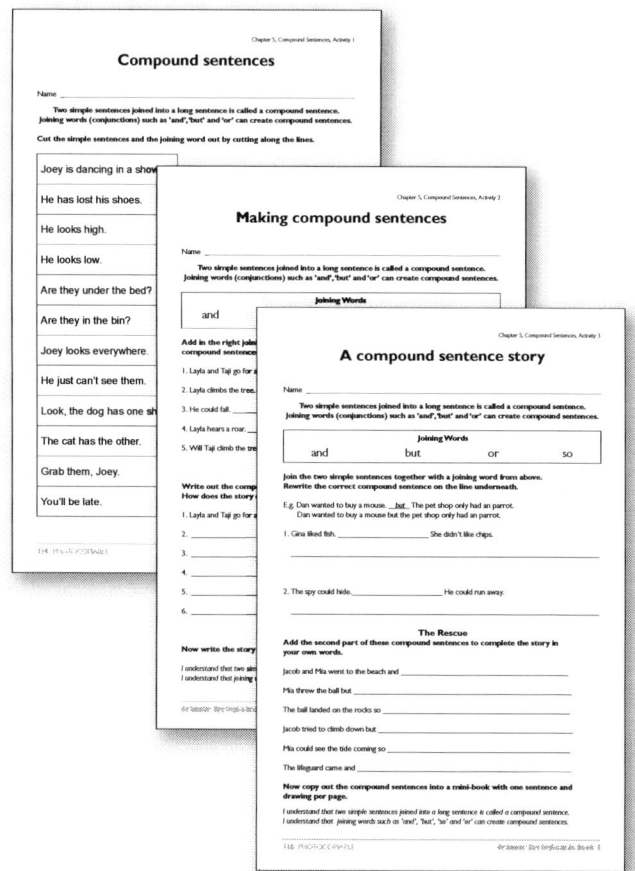

Activities

Group 1

- Lay out the joining words in front of the children and read them out.

- Show the first two short sentences and with the children read them out.

- Ask the children in turn what joining word could be used to turn the sentences into one compound sentence. Write out the correct sentence on the white board or the computer.

- Highlight the omission of the first sentence's full stop and the second sentence's capital letter.

- Do the same procedure with the five other pairs of sentences.

- With the children read out the compound sentences and discuss their effect.

- Give out the mini books and let the children individually either copy the sentences or stick in printed sentences on each page and illustrate the story.

Group 2:

- Give out the activity sheet, 'Making compound sentences' to each child.

- Working individually, the children add in the correct joining word to turn five pairs of simple sentences of a short story into five compound sentences.

- They then write out the compound sentences correctly.

- The children are then asked to finish the story with a compound sentence of their own.

- Once they have finished ask a few questions, e.g. *How did you form the compound sentences? Why did you choose that joining word? How more effective is the story?*

- Give them a mini book to rewrite the story with a compound sentence and picture per page. Let them share their completed books with the group.

Group 3:

- Give out the activity sheet 3, 'A compound sentence story' to each child.

- Working individually, the children add in the best joining word to join a set of simple sentences into two compound sentences.

- They then finish off six compound nouns that tell a story, by adding the last sentence section.

- Once they have finished, discuss with the compound sentences with the children. Ask *'Why did you choose that ending for this compound sentence? Why did you choose that linking word?'*

- Give them a mini book and ask them to rewrite the story with a compound sentence and picture per page.

- If time allow them to share their stories and sentences with the rest of the group.

Plenary:

Before the end of the lesson, bring all the groups together. Ask *'What is a compound sentence? How do we make compound sentences? Give me some examples of a linking word.*

Support:

Write out simple sentences from a well known story and with the children work on joining the sentences up to create compound sentence. Make word wall displays (see Word wall ideas).

Extension:

Encourage the children to create compound sentence poems using joining words such as 'but' or 'so'. Highlight how the first word of a second simple sentence can also be omitted to create more of a flow.

Compound sentences

Name _____

Two simple sentences joined into a long sentence is called a compound sentence. Joining words (conjunctions) such as 'and', 'but' and 'or' can create compound sentences.

Cut the simple sentences and the joining word out by cutting along the lines.

Joey is dancing in a show.
He has lost his shoes.
He looks high.
He looks low.
Are they under the bed?
Are they in the bin?
Joey looks everywhere.
He just can't see them.
Look, the dog has one shoe.
The cat has the other.
Grab them, Joey.
You'll be late.

and
or
but

Making compound sentences

Name _____

**Two simple sentences joined into a long sentence is called a compound sentence.
Joining words (conjunctions) such as 'and', 'but' and 'or' can create compound sentences.**

Joining Words		
and	but	or

Add in the right joining words from above to turn the simple sentences into compound sentences.

1. Layla and Taji go for a walk. _____ They see a tall tree.

2. Layla climbs the tree. _____ Taji is too scared.

3. He could fall. _____ He could get stuck.

4. Layla hears a roar. _____ She sees a lion.

5. Will Taji climb the tree? _____ Will he run away?

**Write out the compound sentences correctly below.
How does the story end? Write the last compound sentence in your own words.**

1. Layla and Taji go for a walk and they see a tall tree.

2. _____

3. _____

4. _____

5. _____

6. _____

Now write the story out in a mini book with one sentence and picture per page.

*I understand that two simple sentences joined into a long sentence is called a compound sentence.
I understand that joining words such as 'and', 'but' and 'or' can create compound sentences.*

A compound sentence story

Name _____

**Two simple sentences joined into a long sentence is called a compound sentence.
Joining words (conjunctions) such as 'and', 'but' and 'or' can create compound sentences.**

Joining Words			
and	but	or	so

**Join the two simple sentences together with a joining word from above.
Rewrite the correct compound sentence on the line underneath.**

E.g. Dan wanted to buy a mouse. __*but*__ The pet shop only had an parrot.
    Dan wanted to buy a mouse but the pet shop only had an parrot.

1. Gina liked fish. _____ She didn't like chips.

_____

2. The spy could hide._____ He could run away.

_____

The Rescue

**Add the second part of these compound sentences to complete the story in
your own words.**

Jacob and Mia went to the beach and _____

Mia threw the ball but _____

The ball landed on the rocks so _____

Jacob tried to climb down but _____

Mia could see the tide coming so _____

The lifeguard came and _____

**Now copy out the compound sentences into a mini-book with one sentence and
drawing per page.**

*I understand that two simple sentences joined into a long sentence is called a compound sentence.
I understand that joining words such as 'and', 'but', 'so' and 'or' can create compound sentences.*

Time Connectives - Time words

Learning Objectives:

- To understand that time words help tell when something is happening in stories and recounts.

- To identify and use time connectives to sequence and connect main parts of a story.

- To write a narrative using time connectives.

Resources

- **Lesson** – 'Chicken Licken' text, 'Chicken Licken pictures'; Time words flash cards- (Lesson resources-CD-ROM).

- **Group 1** – Copies of activity sheet 1, 'My big day' for each child. Colouring pencils.

- **Group 2** — Copies of activity sheet 2.1, 'Space story' and activity sheet 2.2,' Space story pictures and sentences' for each child. Scissors, glue.

- **Group 3** – Copies of activity sheet 3, 'A day in the life of ...' for each child.

Lesson/activity notes

- **Lesson** – In this lesson we have used 'Time words' instead of the term 'Time connectives'. Choose which term is suitable for the skills and understanding of the children. Copy the 'Chicken Licken pictures' before the lesson. After the lesson, the 'Chicken Licken' sentences could be copied or printed out and the pictures coloured in to create a display.

- **Group 1** – The children initially work as a discussion group with teacher support. They work individually on their pictures and may need support in writing sentences.

- **Group 2** – Initial group discussion with teacher/adult. The children then work in pairs on the activity.

- **Group 3** - Initial group discussion with teacher/adult. The children then work in pairs on the activity.

Lesson

Introduction

Display the 'Time words flash cards' for all the children to see. Explain that these words tell when something is happening in stories or everyday life. Choose a simple example of how the time words could be used, e.g. getting up and going to school routine, making a sandwich etc. Write the time sequence sentences out. As you write the sentences, ask the children which time connective could be used to show the right time sequence. Read through the whole sequence.

Main lesson

Explain how time words can also be used to show the order of events in stories. Ask the children to think about the order of events to the traditional tale, 'Chicken Licken' as you read it to them. Once you have read the story, show the 'Chicken Licken pictures' in a mixed up order. Ask the children to put them in the right sequence of events. Point to the time word flash cards and ask the children to recount the story using the time words e.g. *first, then, next, later, finally, afterwards.* Write their sentences under each picture and re-read the story.

Explain to the children that they are going to work on activities that use time connectives. Put the children into their levelled groups and give out the activities. Spend time moving between the groups to discuss individual children's work and assess their level of understanding.

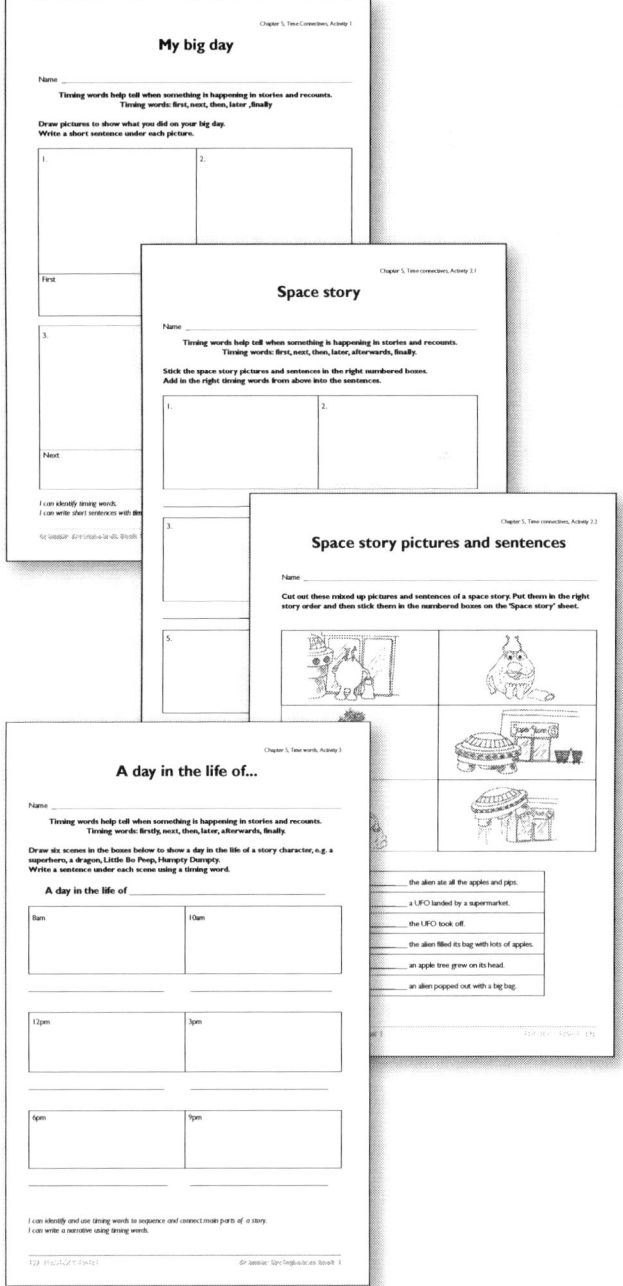

Activities

Group 1

- Give out the activity sheet 1, 'My big day' to each child.

- Working as a group, look at the activity sheet and read out the activity.

- Ask the children to think of a special day and encourage each child to discuss the events in chronological order using the timing words, 'first', 'then', 'next' and finally'.

- Working individually the children then draw their day in the right boxes.

- Act as a scribe or encourage the children to write simple sentences under each picture.

- If time, let the children read out and show their work to the group.

Group 2:

- Give out the activity sheets 'Space story and 'Space story pictures and sentences' to each child.

- With the children read through the definition and the timing word examples on 'Space story 'sheet.

- Highlight that many stories go in time order and discuss examples, e.g. Cinderella.

- Working in pairs, ask the children to cut up the pictures and sentences from 'Space story pictures and sentences' and put them in the right time order.

- Encourage them to read through the story before they stick them on the 'Space story sheet' to see if it makes sense.

- After they have stuck the pictures and sentences down, the children write in the missing timing words in each sentence.

- If time, the children can make up and tell another space story using the timing words and share it with the group.

Group 3

- Give out the activity sheet, 'A day in the life of ...' to each child and put them into pairs.

- As a group, read the definition and the timing word examples with the children.

- Highlight the times in the each picture box and briefly discuss a day of a character as an example.

- Working in pairs, the children decide on their character and draw pictures of its day on their activity sheets.

- They then write sentences under each picture using the timing words from a list.

- Once they have finished, encourage the children to share their work with other children in their group.

Plenary:

Before the end of the lesson, bring all the groups together. Ask some of the children to read and share their work with the class. Write the timing words on a board as the children read out their sentences. Discuss how they help the reader and writer know when an event or something is happening.

Support:

Look at other simple stories with a clear sequence of events. Encourage the children to draw pictures to show the sequence and write the timing words under each one. Display and discuss the story.

Extension

Highlight how time words can also be used in instructions on doing something. Let the children draw and write simple instructions using time words for making a wacky sandwich or amazing snack.

My big day

Name _____

Timing words help tell when something is happening in stories and recounts.
Timing words: first, next, then, later ,finally

Draw pictures to show what you did on your big day.
Write a short sentence under each picture.

1. First	2. Then
3. Next	4. Finally

I can identify timing words.
I can write short sentences with timing words.

Space story

Name _____

Timing words help tell when something is happening in stories and recounts.
Timing words: first, next, then, later, afterwards, finally.

Stick the space story pictures and sentences in the right numbered boxes.
Add in the right timing words from above into the sentences.

1.	2.

_____   _____

3.	4.

_____   _____

5.	6.

_____   _____

I can identify and use timing words to sequence and connect main parts of a story.
I can write a narrative using timing words.

Space story pictures and sentences

Name _____

Cut out these mixed up pictures and sentences of a space story. Put them in the right story order and then stick them in the numbered boxes on the 'Space story' sheet.

_____ the alien ate all the apples and pips.
_____ a UFO landed by a supermarket.
_____ the UFO took off.
_____ the alien filled its bag with lots of apples.
_____ an apple tree grew on its head.
_____ an alien popped out with a big bag.

A day in the life of...

Name _____

Timing words help tell when something is happening in stories and recounts.
Timing words: firstly, next, then, later, afterwards, finally.

Draw six scenes in the boxes below to show a day in the life of a story character, e.g. a superhero, a dragon, Little Bo Peep, Humpty Dumpty.
Write a sentence under each scene using a timing word.

A day in the life of _____

8am	10am

_____   _____

12pm	3pm

_____   _____

6pm	9pm

_____   _____

I can identify and use timing words to sequence and connect main parts of a story.
I can write a narrative using timing words.

Prepositions (position words)

Learning Objectives:
- To understand that position words tell where something or someone is or gives directions.

- To identify and use position words.

Resources
- **Lesson** – 'Position word flash cards',

- **Group 1** – Copies of 'Where is the treasure?' for each child. Colouring pencils, scissors, glue.

- **Group 2** — Copies of 'Captain Pip's treasure island' for each child. Colouring pencils.

- **Group 3** – Copies of 'Pirate Pip's treasure cave' for each child. Colouring pencils.

Lesson/activity notes
- **Lesson** – To make the lesson activity more interesting, you may want to put unusual objects or pictures around the classroom for the children to focus on.

- **Group 1** – Children work as a discussion group then individually on the activity with teacher adult support.

- **Group 2** – Children work individually on the activity.

- **Group 3** – Children work individually and then swap work with a partner.

Lesson

Introduction
Display the 'Position word flash cards' so that all the children can see them. With the children read through the words. Explain that these words tell where something or someone is. Give a quick example, e.g. *I am standing in front of the board*. Write out the sentence and underline the position word, 'front'.

Main lesson
Point and read out the first position word. Ask the children to look around the classroom and tell you a sentence of where something or someone is using that position word. Write down several of their sentences as examples. Do the same procedure going through each position words. With the children, read through them. Discuss how position words can be useful in non-fiction writing- information texts, recounts, giving directions and in stories e.g. tells where a character, place or object is.

Explain to the children that they are going to work on activities using position words. Put the children into their levelled groups and give out the activities. Spend time moving between the groups to discuss individual children's work and assess their level of understanding.

Activities

Group 1
- Give out copies of 'Where is the treasure?' to each child.

- Read out the instructions with the children.

- Let them cut out the sentences and help them read out the sentences.

- Ask them to underline the position words with a pencil.

- The children look at the pictures and stick the correct sentences each one.

- Finally they can draw a picture to go with the last clue.

- When they have finished, discuss how difficult it would have been to find the treasure if the positional words were not in the sentences.

Group 2
- Give out copies of 'Captain Pip's treasure island' to each child.

- Working individually, the children read the treasure clues and underline the position words in each sentence.

- They then add three more clues of their own clues using position words from a list.

- Finally they draw in the places from the clues onto a treasure map.

- When they have finished, discuss how difficult it would have been to find the treasure if the positional words were not in the sentences.

Group 3:

- Give out copies of 'Captain Pip's treasure cave' to each child.

- Working individually, the children draw treasures from a treasure list onto a treasure cave scene, using a list of position words to decide where each one should go.

- They then pass their sheet to a partner who completes the six sentences at the end by studying the completed picture.

- The children then pair-share their findings with each other.

- When they have finished, discuss the use of position words when trying to show or explain where something or someone is.

Plenary:

Before the end of the lesson, bring the groups together. Ask the children from each group to read out different examples of sentences using position words. Write a few on the board. Revise how position words tell where something or someone is in a sentence. If time, play a game of Hot or Cold (see Sentence Spring board)

Support:

Create a treasure hunt around the school or in the playground. Give instructions verbally or in simple sentences to small groups. At the end ask them what position words were used.

Extension:

Let the children look at pictures or photographs of places. Ask them to write five questions about where objects, people or places are in the picture using position words, e.g. 'What is in front of the house?' To make it harder, turn it into a memory game.

Where is the treasure?

Name _____

Position words tell where something or someone is or gives directions,
e.g. *The ball is on the table. The ball is under the table.*

Help Pirate Pip find his treasure by cutting out the clues and sticking them under the
right pictures. Draw a picture for the last clue.

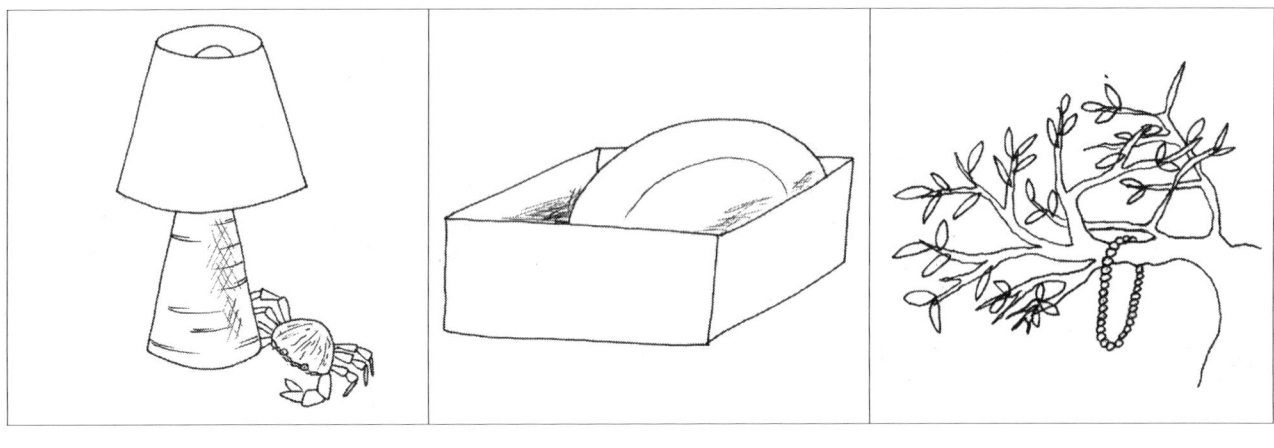

_____   _____   _____

_____   _____   The ring is beside the shell.

The necklace is up in the tree.	The lamp is by the crab.
The crown is on the sandcastle.	The cup is under the bush.
	The plate is inside the box.

Captain Pip's treasure island

Name _____

Position words tell where something or someone is or gives directions,
e.g. *The ball is on the table. The ball is under the table.*

Help Pirate Pip find the treasure by underlining the position words in these clues.
Add in three more clues at the end using these position words.

under   next   on

Walk <u>across</u> the sandy beach.

Climb up the rocky hill.

Roll down the muddy slope.

Skip beside the swampy pool.

Crawl behind the little waterfall.

Tiptoe in front of the snappy crocs.

Look below the bendy coconut tree.

_____

_____

_____

Now add in the places on the pirate map.

I understand that position words tell where something or someone is or gives directions.
I can identify and use position words.

Grammar Springboards Book 1

Pirate Pip's treasure cave

Name _____

Position words tell where something or someone is or gives directions,
e.g. *The ball is on the table. The ball is under the table.*

Draw in treasures from the 'Treasures' list to the picture below.
Use the 'Position words' to help you decide where the treasures should be placed.
Then pass this sheet to your partner and ask them to complete the six sentences below
by looking at your picture.

| **Position** |
| In front |
| behind |
| next |
| under |
| above |
| on |

| **Treasures** |
| necklace |
| crown |
| ring |
| coins |
| gold plate |
| jewelled cup |

Use the picture to add in the missing position words and objects of the
sentences below.

1. The necklace is _____ the _____.

2. The crown is _____ the _____.

3. The ring is _____ the _____.

4. The coins are _____ the _____.

5. The gold plate is _____ the _____.

6. The jewelled cup is _____ the _____.

I understand that position words tell where something or someone is or gives directions.
I can identify and use position words.

Chapter 6 – Punctuation
Punctuation information

Questions
Questions are sentences that ask something and expect an answer.
All questions end with a question mark (?).

There are several types of questions:
1. Interrogative questions, which are questions that mainly start with wh-words
   E.g. when, where, who, what, why, how, which.
   - 'What' is used when questions are asked about things.
   - 'Who' is used when questions are asked about people.
   - 'When' is used when questions are asked about time.
   - 'Where' is used when questions are asked about places.
   - 'Why' is used when questions are asked to find a reason.
   - 'Which' is used when questions are asked about a choice.
   - 'How' is used when questions are asked to find out about things and people.

2. Tag questions are questions that start with a statement and have a question tagged onto the end.
   E.g. He is funny, isn't he?

3. A yes / no question is a question that can only have a yes or no answer.
   E.g. Are you happy? Yes.

4. An alternative question is a question which gives more than two answers within the question.
   E.g. Would you like water, juice, coffee or tea?

Full stops (.) Full stops are used at the end of sentences.

Exclamation marks (!) Exclamations are used to make a point, speaking with force or show surprise. They are usually used in a short sentence.
E.g. Look out! I can't do it! That is amazing!

Speech marks ("_") Speech marks show speech within writing.
E.g. "I wish I could go home," sighed Jake.

Commas (,) Commas can be used for different purposes:
1. To separate words in a list within a sentence. They take the place of the word 'and' and 'or' in a list of more than three words and phrases. The last word in the list has 'and' or 'or' before it.
   E.g. In my bag I have a pen, book, purse, phone, tissues and a lipstick.

2. To separate the spoken word from the unspoken word at the end of a piece of written dialogue.
   E.g. "Look at Mo dance," laughed Frankie.

3. To separate clauses such as a beginning clause in a sentence.
   E.g. Later that night, Ava sat down and ate her tea.

4. To separate a clause or phrase that offers extra information within a sentence.
   E.g. Grandma, who was nearly ninety, kicked the ball into the goal.

Punctuation Springboards

Word walls

Create eye catching word walls. One flash card equals one brick. Have several bricks to create the word wall with the children. Have blank cards that the children can write new words and add to or make a new word wall shape.

The walls can be used in a variety of ways.

* **Questions:** have a short question on a brick and an answer on each brick. Do several and encourage the children to match them up. Have a wall for the question words e.g. what, when, which, where, why, how.

* **Commas:** have a wall of objects which the children can use to make up lists using commas.

* **Punctuation sign wall:** have punctuation signs in a wall as reference for the children and discussion points.

The Word ladder

A similar game to 'Consequences'. In groups of four the children are given strips of paper with four sections (see Word ladder Template – Teacher resources). The children write a word or sentence on the first section, fold over the paper to hide it and pass it to the next child. They then write another word or sentence on the next and so on. After the strip has been completed it is opened up and the children read out the four written words or sentences.

* **Questions** - The game can be used for questions. The first section is a question followed by an answer then a question and then an answer. The children read out the fun results.

* **Commas** - The children write words to create a list. They write out their final lists adding in commas.

* **Speech marks** - Speech sentences with speech marks can make a fun dialogue.

Write a speech

The children are given bits of paper. They write one or two pieces of dialogue on the paper with speech marks. The pieces of paper are all put in a box/hat. They are shuffled and as a group or class the lines are put into some form of sequence for a fun dialogue story which is read out loud.

Other activities

* Who am I? What am I? Where am I? Question games.

* Yes and no question.

* Write pairs of cards, e.g. male and female names of animals, two parts of a compound noun. The children are given one card and they have to ask other children questions to find their matching pair.

* Joke and riddle books or displays.

* Play question rhyme games e.g. What's the time, Mr Wolf?

* Collect a list of class questions. Each child contributes a question that they would like to find the answer. The questions are written out with the children.

* Make collections of things that could relate to a topic or specific children's interests e.g. stamp collecting, mini-beasts, marbles, trump cards etc. Encourage the children to write lists of the collections.

* Have a washing line with objects and words and get the children to create lists.

* Cut out speech bubbles from comics and get the children to rewrite the speech in their own words using speech marks.

* Fun lists and menus.

Questions

Learning Objectives:

- To understand that a question sentence ends with a question mark

- To understand that questions usually have an answer.

- To recognise that questions often start with what, when, who, where, which, why, how.

- To write simple questions and answers.

Resources:

- **Lesson** – 'Question word flash cards', (Teacher resources- CD-ROM), whiteboard.

- **Group 1** – Copies of activity sheet 1, 'A Busy Street' for each child or a picture/photo of a busy scene e.g. a Bruegel or Lowry painting. 'Question words flash cards' (Teacher resources – CD-ROM), a bag, whiteboard (small or large).

- **Group 2** – Copies of activity sheet 2, 'Tell me a joke' for each child. Joke books.

- **Group 3** – Copies of activity sheet 3.1 'A quiz' and activity sheet 3.2 'My quiz' for each child, spare paper, books, and resources on fiction or non-fiction topics.

Lesson/activity notes

- **Lesson** – Copy and cut up the 'Question word flash cards' before the lesson.

- **Group 1** – Children work as a group with teacher/adult support. Put the 'Question words flash cards' into the bag before the activity. Use the activity picture or a painting/picture of a busy scene.

- **Group 2** – Children work individually on matching the jokes and then with a partner to create two jokes.

- **Group 3** – Children work individually on activity sheet 3.1, 'A quiz'. They work in pairs on activity sheet 3.2, 'My quiz'.

Lesson

Introduction

Start the lesson by playing, 'Twenty questions'. Explain that you are an object or a story character and the children have to ask up to twenty questions to guess what or who you are. At the end of the game, highlight that questions are sentences that ask something. Write one of the questions the children asked on the board. Highlight the use of a question mark instead of a full stop. Display the 'Question words flash cards' for all the children to see. Read through each word and explain that they often start a question.

Main Lesson

Choose a favourite book character such as Cinderella and ask the children to think of seven questions they would like to ask her using the seven question words. Write out examples of some of the children's suggestions. E.g. *Where do you go on holiday? What is your favourite sweet? Who is your best friend?* As you write the questions out, reinforce the use of the question mark at the end. Ask the children to work in small groups to think of simple answers for each question. After a few minutes, write down their answers. Highlight, the repeated word pattern in the answers, e.g. *My favourite sweet is chocolate.*

Explain to the children that they are going to work on activities on questions. Put the children into their levelled groups and give out the activities. Spend time moving between the groups to discuss individual children's work and assess their level of understanding.

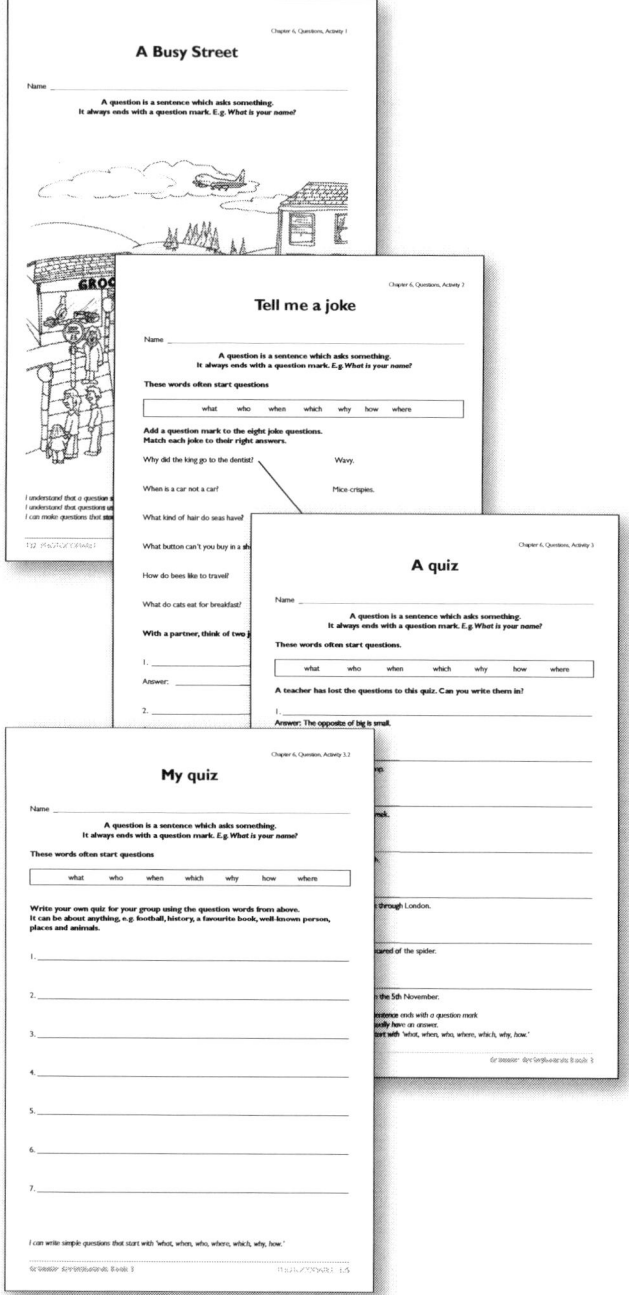

Activities

Group 1
- Give out copies of activity sheet 1, 'A busy street' to each child.

- Put the 'Question words flash cards' in a bag in the middle of the table. Then ask a child to take a card and say it out loud.

- They then look at 'A busy street' and use it to ask a question beginning with their question word, e.g. Where is the cat?

- Write out the question on a whiteboard and ask *'What should a question end with?'*

- Once the children have answered the question, the question card is put back in the bag and the next child repeats the procedure.

- When all the children have asked a question, read through the questions and highlight the question mark.

- Allow the children to colour in the picture, encouraging them to think of other questions they could ask.

Group 2:
- Give out the copies activity sheet 2, 'Tell me a joke' to each of the children.

- Highlight that jokes are questions with funny answers.

- Working individually, the children match the joke question to the right answer and then add the question marks.

- Finally they work with a partner to write two of their own jokes.

- Allow the children to share their jokes with the rest of the group.

- If time, challenge each pair to write a riddle question for another pair to solve.

Group 3:
- Give out copies of 'A quiz' and 'My quiz' to each child.

- Working individually, the children write the missing questions to written answers for a quiz on activity sheet 3.1.'A quiz'.

- They then work in pairs on activity sheet 3.2, 'My quiz' to write seven questions for a quiz of their own choice, e.g. a favourite hobby or subject.

- Allow the children access to books and resources to help them put together their questions.

- Encourage them to write out their questions in rough before they add them to the sheet. Check if they have added a question mark.

- Allow the children to swop their quizzes with other pairs of children.

Plenary:
Before the end of the lesson, bring all the groups together. Encourage the children to share the questions they used in their activities. Write a few more examples of questions in the board and reinforce the use of question marks and use of the question words. If time, have a quick class quiz or collect more jokes from the children.

Support:
To reinforce the idea of questions, have a drama hot seat session where the children can ask a story character questions. Work as a scribe to help them record their questions. Let them add in the question marks and underline the questions words.

Extension:
Encourage the children to use questions in their topic or class work. They could create a simple questionnaire or survey about improving the school environment or supporting the 3Rs, write a quiz for the class, design book review question sheets.

A Busy Street

Name _____

A question is a sentence which asks something.
It always ends with a question mark. E.g. *What is your name?*

I understand that a question sentence ends with a question mark.
I understand that questions usually have an answer.
I can make questions that start with 'what, when, who, where, which, why, how'

Tell me a joke

Name _____

A question is a sentence which asks something.
It always ends with a question mark. *E.g. What is your name?*

These words often start questions

| what | who | when | which | why | how | where |

Add a question mark to the eight joke questions.
Match each joke to their right answers.

Why did the king go to the dentist?　　　　　　　Wavy.

When is a car not a car?　　　　　　　Mice-crispies.

What kind of hair do seas have?　　　　　　　A belly button.

What button can't you buy in a shop?　　　　　　　To get his teeth crowned.

How do bees like to travel?　　　　　　　When it turns into a garage.

What do cats eat for breakfast?　　　　　　　By buzz.

With a partner, think of two jokes and write them below. Share them with friends.

1. _____

Answer: _____

2. _____

Answer: _____

I can understand that a question sentence ends with a question mark
I can understand that questions usually have an answer.
I can write simple questions that start with 'what, when, who, where, which, why, how.'

A quiz

Name _____

A question is a sentence which asks something.
It always ends with a question mark. *E.g. What is your name?*

These words often start questions.

what	who	when	which	why	how	where

A teacher has lost the questions to this quiz. Can you write them in?

1. _____

Answer: The opposite of big is small.

2. _____

Answer: Aladdin had a magic lamp.

3. _____

Answer: There are 7 days in a week.

4. _____

Answer: Worms live in the earth.

5. _____

Answer: The River Thames runs through London.

6. _____

Answer: Little Miss Muffet was scared of the spider.

7. _____

Answer: Guy Fawkes Night is on the 5th November.

I can understand that a question sentence ends with a question mark
I can understand that questions usually have an answer.
I can write simple questions that start with 'what, when, who, where, which, why, how.'

My quiz

Name _____

**A question is a sentence which asks something.
It always ends with a question mark. *E.g. What is your name?***

These words often start questions

what	who	when	which	why	how	where

**Write your own quiz for your group using the question words from above.
It can be about anything, e.g. football, history, a favourite book, well-known person,
places and animals.**

1. _____

2. _____

3. _____

4. _____

5. _____

6. _____

7. _____

I can write simple questions that start with 'what, when, who, where, which, why, how.'

Commas in lists

Learning Objectives:

- To understand the use of commas replacing 'and' in sentences containing lists.

- To add commas accurately into sentences containing lists.

- To write sentences with commas in lists.

Resources:

- **Lesson** – Whiteboard for all the children to see.

- **Group 1** – Copy and cut activity sheets 1, 'Object cards' and activity sheet 1.2 'Commas/and flash cards'. A box to put the cards in. A whiteboard or display board.

- **Group 2** – Copies of activity sheet 2, 'Nature trail lists' for each child.

- **Group 3** – Copies of activity sheet 3, 'The Story Book Ball' to each child.

Lesson/activity notes

- **Group 1** – Children work as a discussion group with teacher/adult support.

- **Group 2** – Children work individually on the activity and then in pairs create a nature list. Teacher discussion during the activity.

- **Group 3** – Children work individually on the activity with teacher discussion at the beginning and the end. The children share their lists with the group.

Explain to the children that they are going to work on activities on commas in lists.

Put the children into their levelled groups and give out the activities. Spend time moving between the groups to discuss individual children's work and assess their level of understanding.

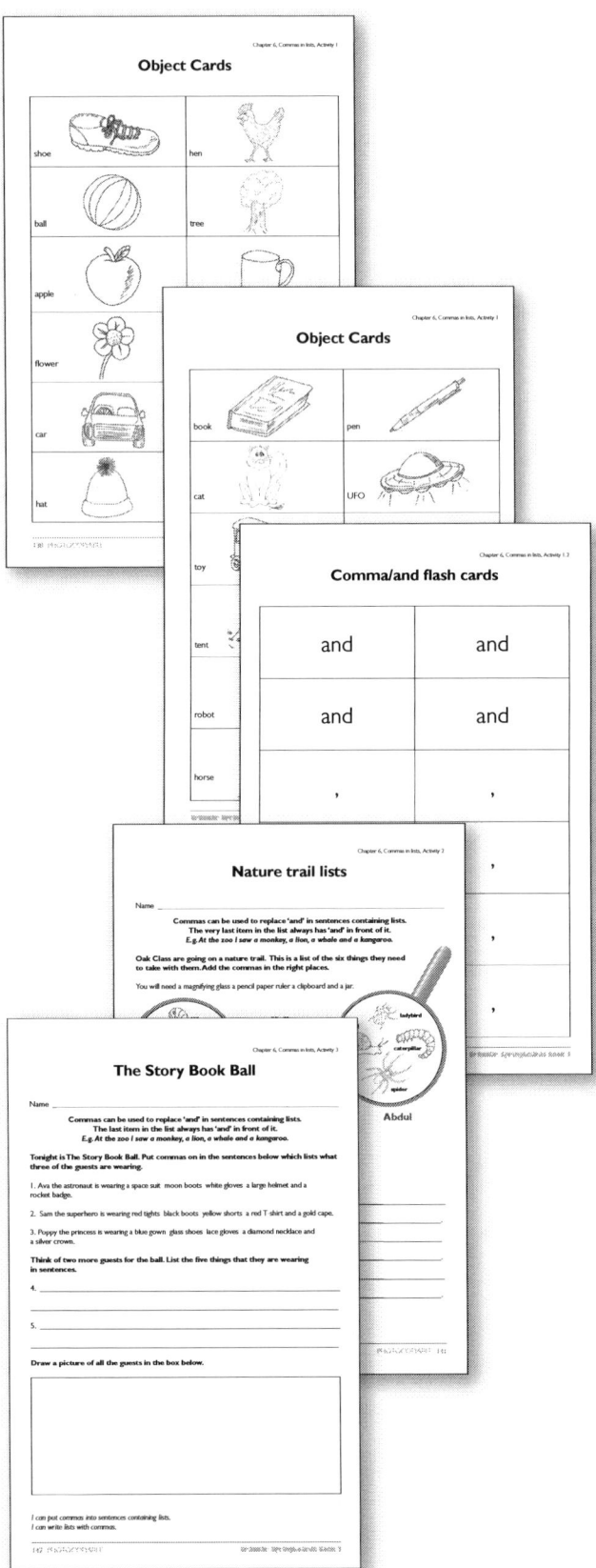

Lesson

Introduction

Start the lesson playing 'When I went shopping I bought...' game with the children. Write *'When I went shopping I bought'* on the board and then write each item along the board with an 'and' between each item as each child contributes their idea, e.g. *When I went shopping I bought a hat and a skirt and a bag of sweets and a...'* Put a limit of about ten items and then stop the game

Main lesson

Read out the first sentence to the children, emphasising the word 'and'. Highlight that the sentence is a long shopping list. Highlight all the 'and' in the sentence. Discuss how they make the sentence sound long and awkward. Introduce and draw a comma on the board. Explain to the children that it can be used to replace the 'and's. Rub out each 'and' in the list and replace it with a comma. Stop at the last item and emphasis that the very last item keeps the 'and'. Read out the list with commas with the children and discuss the improvement.

Activities

Group 1

- Put a box with the set of 'Object cards' in the middle of the table. Have the pile of 'Commas/'and flash cards' by the box.

- Explain to the children that working as a group they are going to make a list of the objects in the box using commas.

- Start the game by saying *'In the box there is a...'*

- A child takes a card out of the box, says what the object is e.g. 'shoe' and lays it on the table. They then put a comma card after it.

- The group then say *'In the box there is a shoe,'* and the next child adds to the list.

- When the last card comes out, reinforce that the 'and' card is used to end the list.

- Read out the list with the children and display the cards with commas or re-write on a board.

Group 2:

- Give out the copies of activity sheet 2 'Nature trail lists' to each child.

- Working individually, the children add commas into a list of items needed for a nature trail.

- They then write out three lists of what three children found in the nature trail.

- Once they have completed the activity ask the children why commas are used in lists instead of 'and'.

- If time ask them to work in pairs to compile a list of other creatures, flowers or trees that they might see on a nature trail.

- Encourage them to share their lists with others in their group.

Group 3:

- Give out the copies of activity sheet 3, 'The Story Book Ball' to each child.

- Working individually, the children add commas into three sentences which list what three guests are wearing.

- Before they start, highlight that each item on the lists has an adjective describing it so the children need to think carefully where they put the commas.

- Once they have completed the activity, they create two more guests and list the five items that the guests are wearing. Encourage the use of adjectives in the lists.

- The children can then draw a picture of all the guests using the lists as information.

- Once they have finished encourage the children to compare their last two lists.

Plenary:

Before the end of the lesson, bring all the groups together. Encourage the children to share the lists they worked on in their activities. Write a couple on the whiteboard without commas and ask the children where the commas should go. Highlight the use of 'and' to signal the end of the list. If time have one more oral game of *'When I went to...'* with the children.

Support:

To help children understand the use of a comma in a list, work more with picture/words and the comma flash cards or bring in actual objects for different topics, e.g. ingredients for a sandwich, lists of animals in a zoo, objects in the art area.

Extension:

Extending on from the worksheet, highlight that lists in sentences don't have to be just single words but one or two words e.g. describing a noun, 'a golden spade or a verb and noun, 'a jumping frog.' Encourage the children to explore and create fun and unusual lists,

Object Cards

shoe	hen
ball	tree
apple	mug
flower	cake
car	carrot
hat	ring

Object Cards

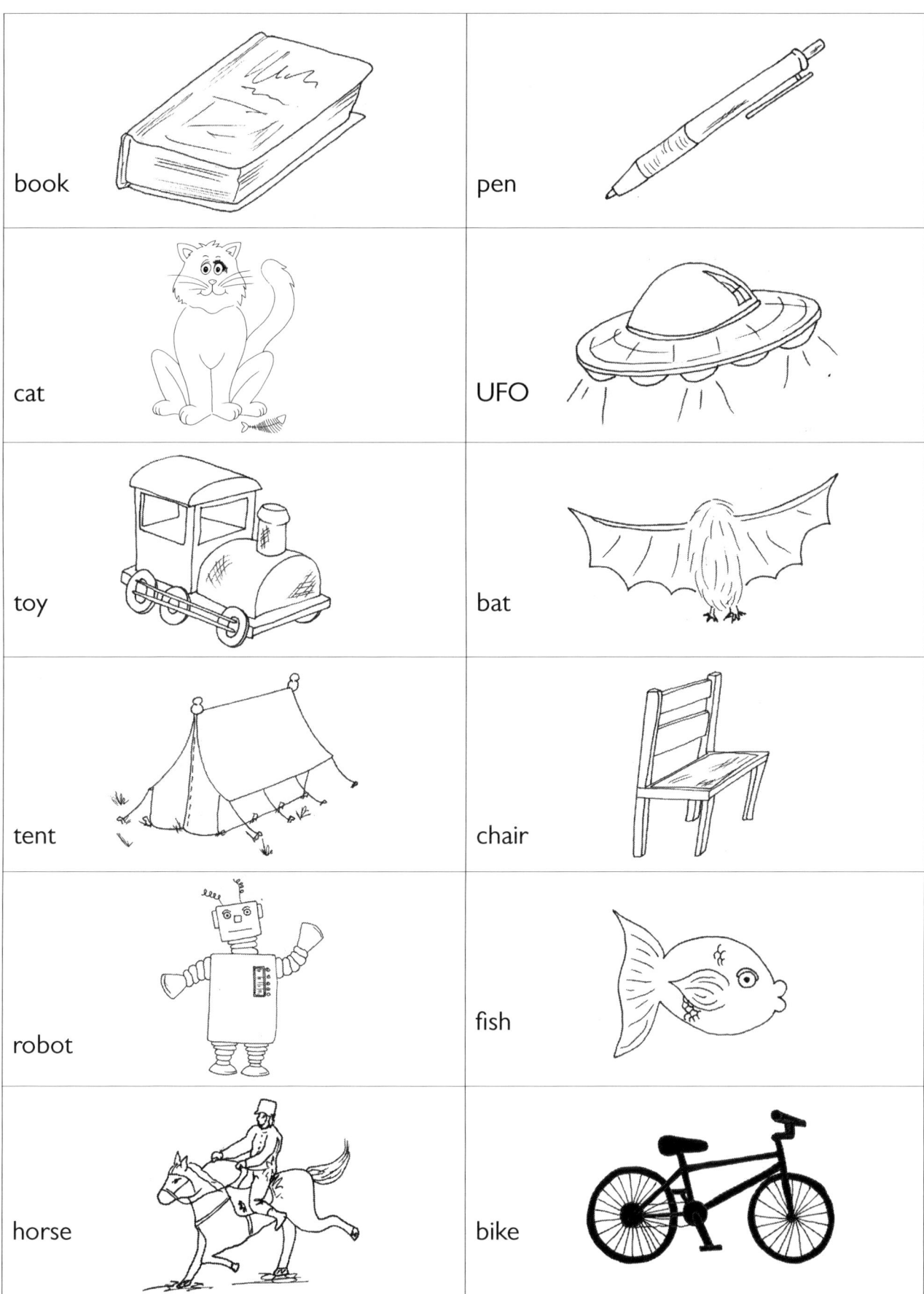

book

pen

cat

UFO

toy

bat

tent

chair

robot

fish

horse

bike

Comma/and flash cards

and	and
and	and
,	,
,	,
,	,
,	,

Nature trail lists

Name _____

Commas can be used to replace 'and' in sentences containing lists.
The very last item in the list always has 'and' in front of it.
E.g. At the zoo I saw a monkey, a lion, a whale and a kangaroo.

Oak Class are going on a nature trail. This is a list of the six things they need to take with them. Add the commas in the right places.

You will need a magnifying glass a pencil paper ruler a clipboard and a jar.

Kelly

Worm

Beetle

Earwig

Ant

Jonah

acorn

oak leaf

feather

pine cone

ladybird

snail

caterpillar

spider

Abdul

Write a list of what Kelly, Abdul and Jonah found.

Kelly found a_____

_____.

Abdul found a_____

_____.

Jonah found a_____

_____.

I can put commas into sentences containing lists.
I can write lists with commas.

The Story Book Ball

Name _____

**Commas can be used to replace 'and' in sentences containing lists.
The last item in the list always has 'and' in front of it.
E.g. At the zoo I saw a monkey, a lion, a whale and a kangaroo.**

Tonight is The Story Book Ball. Put commas on in the sentences below which lists what three of the guests are wearing.

1. Ava the astronaut is wearing a space suit moon boots white gloves a large helmet and a rocket badge.

2. Sam the superhero is wearing red tights black boots yellow shorts a red T-shirt and a gold cape.

3. Poppy the princess is wearing a blue gown glass shoes lace gloves a diamond necklace and a silver crown.

Think of two more guests for the ball. List the five things that they are wearing in sentences.

4. _____

_____

5. _____

_____

Draw a picture of all the guests in the box below.

I can put commas into sentences containing lists.
I can write lists with commas.

Speech marks

bridge' said Little Billy Goat Gruff. Highlight that something is needed to show Little Billy Goat Gruff's spoken words. Introduce the 'Speech mark flash cards' and explain that they show when a character is talking in a sentence. Note that the first speech mark looks like the number '66'. Add the speech mark at the beginning of the speech. Ask where 'Little Billy Goat Gruff' finishes speaking. Add in the second speech mark and note that it looks like the number, '99'. Rewrite all the speech bubble texts with the children adding the right punctuation. Model the commas, question marks and exclamation marks to show that they come before the last speech marks. Read through the story and discuss how speech marks make a difference.

Explain to the children that they are going to work on activities on speech marks. Put the children into their levelled groups and give out the activities. Spend time moving between the groups to discuss individual children's work and assess their level of understanding.

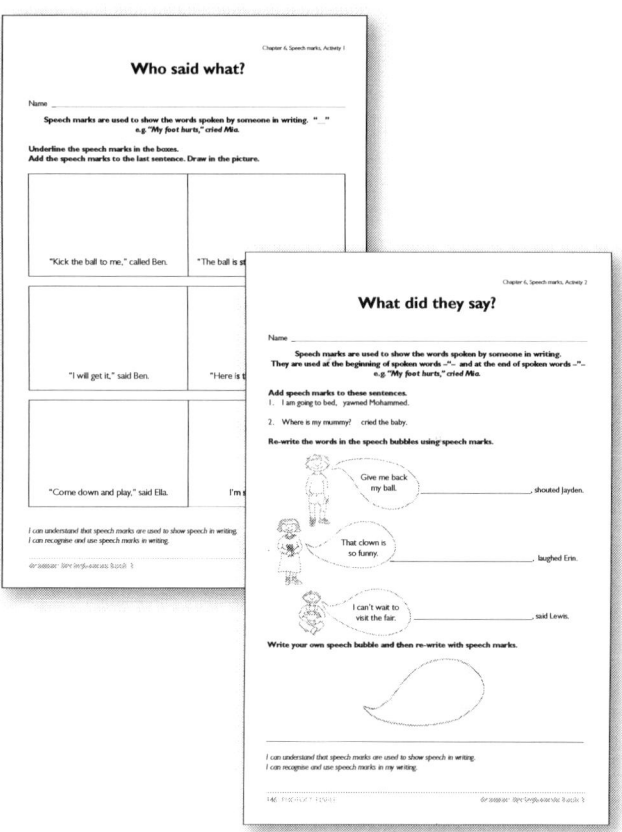

Lesson

Introduction

Start the lesson by telling the children the story of 'Three Billy Goats Gruff.' Afterwards explain that the story is going to be acted out using just the characters spoken words. Choose four children to play the four characters. Display the 'Speech bubble dialogue cards' for them to read or if a child has reading difficulties tell them the dialogue. After the children have acted out the story, highlight that speech bubbles are used in comics but most of the time, characters spoken words are written within sentences.

Main lesson

Re-write the first speech bubble text on a board. Add the character's name to make a sentence, e.g. *'I'm going over the old*

Activities

Group 1

- Give out copies of activity sheet 1, 'Who said what?' to each child.

- With the children read out the dialogue sentences.

- Ask them to underline the speech marks in the sentences.

- Let them add their own speech marks on the last two sentences and draw pictures for all the sentences.

- At the end of the activity, encourage the children to take turns reading out the speech marked part of the sentences with expression.

Group 2:

- Give out copies of activity sheet 2, 'What did they say?' to each child.

- Working individually, the children add speech marks into two sentences.

- They then re-write the words in three speech bubbles using speech marks.

- Finally they write a simple speech bubble and then re-write underneath using speech marks.

- Once they have finished the activity, highlight the use of different 'said' words to indicate the mood or feelings of a character.

- If time, let the children look at story books to identify speech marks and ways that the writers highlight the feelings and moods of the characters.

Group 3:

- Put the children into twos or threes and give them paper and 'Speech bubbles'.

- Give each group a scene from a well known traditional story such as Little Red Riding Hood, The Little Red Hen, The Magic Porridge Pot.

- Ask the children to write the spoken words into the speech bubbles.

- Once they have written these out, discuss how they would write out the words using speech marks.

- Model re-writing the words as a sentence using speech marks and the words indicating who said the words.

- Let the children re-write their words and then let another small group read out their work.

Plenary

Before the end of the lesson, bring all the groups together. Encourage the children to share their work with the other groups. Use a big book to highlight examples of speech marks in writing. Highlight how they look like 66 and 99.

Support:

Create a short fictional scene of a chosen genre, e.g. fantasy, everyday. Let each child be a chosen character. Start the scene, e.g. *Where can we go to get the Dragon's Pearl?'* Write or record the speech. The children then take turns saying something in response to the last speech. Write out the whole scene and let the children help you add in the speech marks.

Extension:

Let the children create their own stories using speech marks. Give them a word list of 'said' words to help them make their speech words interesting. Discuss and encourage the use of exclamation marks to highlight something exciting happening.

Who said what?

Name _____

Speech marks are used to show the words spoken by someone in writing. "___"
e.g. "My foot hurts," cried Mia.

Underline the speech marks in the boxes.
Add the speech marks to the last sentence. Draw in the picture.

"Kick the ball to me," called Ben.	"The ball is stuck in the tree," said Ella.
"I will get it," said Ben.	"Here is the ball," shouted Ben.
"Come down and play," said Ella.	I'm stuck! cried Ben.

I can understand that speech marks are used to show speech in writing.
I can recognise and use speech marks in writing.

What did they say?

Name _____

**Speech marks are used to show the words spoken by someone in writing.
They are used at the beginning of spoken words –"– and at the end of spoken words –"–
e.g. *"My foot hurts," cried Mia.***

Add speech marks to these sentences.

1.   I am going to bed,   yawned Mohammed.

2.   Where is my mummy?   cried the baby.

Re-write the words in the speech bubbles using speech marks.

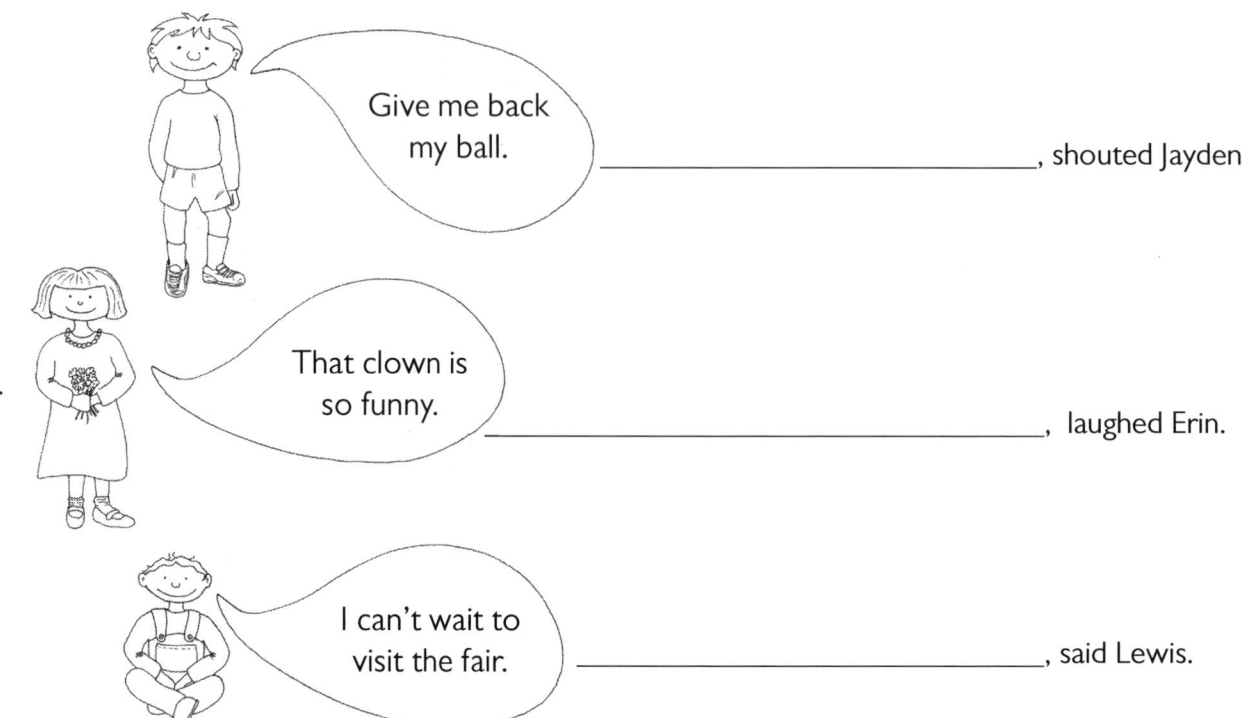

Give me back my ball.

_____, shouted Jayden.

That clown is so funny.

_____, laughed Erin.

I can't wait to visit the fair.

_____, said Lewis.

Write your own speech bubble and then re-write with speech marks.

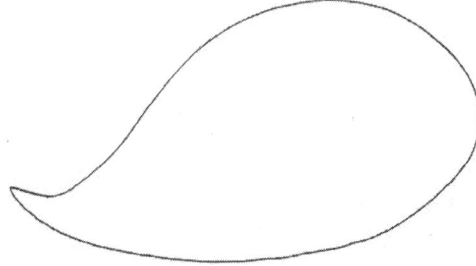

_____

I can understand that speech marks are used to show speech in writing.
I can recognise and use speech marks in my writing.

Contents

Periodic Assessment tests

Test 1 - Nouns   148

Test 2 - Nouns   150

Test 1 - Pronouns   152

Test 2 - Pronouns   154

Test 1 - Verbs   156

Test 2 - Verbs   158

Test 1 - Adjectives   160

Test 2 - Adjectives   162

Test 1 - Sentences   164

Test 2 - Sentences   166

Test 1 - Punctuation   168

Test 2 - Punctuation   170

Transitional Assessment tests

Transitional test 1   172

Transitional test 2   178

Assessment Charts

Writing Assessment chart 185

Reading Assessment chart 187

Periodic Assessment test 1 – Nouns

Name: _____

Date: _____

Class: _____

Level: _____

1. Which word is the odd one out? Circle the word that is not a noun.

dog	jumping	shop	cup

2. Underline the nouns in the sentences.

a. The cat ran away.

b. I went to the park.

c. I have lost a sock.

d. The clown was funny.

3. Circle the proper nouns.

a. I was born in May.

b. My best friend is called Becky.

c. I went to London and saw Big Ben.

4. Re-write the proper nouns with a capital letter.

emily   _____

harry   _____

sunday   _____

world cup _____

tesco   _____

5. Match the two words and write their compound nouns.

arm	sun	foot
ball	chair	flower

a. _____

b. _____

c. _____

6. Write the compound nouns from the noun words and pictures

a.

      hand   +   bag   = _____

b.

      Jelly   +   fish   = _____

7. Turn these nouns into plurals (more than one thing).

shell   boot   cat   sock

_____   _____   _____   _____

8. Add a plural to the nouns in the sentences.

a. The girl used the pen ___.

b. The giant put on his shoe ____.

c. The dog ____ barked all day.

9. Add 'an' or 'a' in front of these nouns.

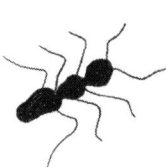         

____ ant   ____ hat   ____ owl   ____ tree

10. Underline the 'an' and 'a' in these sentences.

a. I jumped over a gate.

b. Sita saw ____ elephant.

c. Mrs Way gave me _____ ruler.

d. I would like ____ ice cream.

e. I need ____ umbrella.

Periodic Assessment test 2 – Nouns

Name: _____

Date: _____

Class: _____

Level: _____

1. Underline the common nouns in these sentences.

    a. Joe went to the river and caught a fish.

    b. The alien flew to the blue planet.

    c. The frog jumped on a rock.

2. Add nouns to complete the sentences.

    a. I ran down the _____.

    b. In the jungle I saw a huge hairy _____.

    c. Have you meet my _____.

    d. I am off to swim at the _____.

3. Underline the proper nouns in the sentence. Circle the capital letters.

    a. I live along King's Street.

    b. My uncle is going to Canada.

    c. Thea's party is next Saturday.

    d. Mrs Brooks runs the Jumping Gym Club.

4. Write two sentences using these proper nouns.   Shrek   Australia

_____

_____

5. Match the nouns to make and write four compound nouns.

cow	rain	lip	hand
stick	bag	boy	bow

_____   _____

_____   _____

6. Write two sentences using these compound nouns.

_____

_____

7. Write the plurals of the nouns in the box.

shell	shells
sock	
plate	
boat	
castle	
flower	

8. Turn the nouns in the sentences into plurals.

a. Katy put the stone__ on her sandcastle.

b. Dad washed the cup____ and saucer_____.

c. Rob wanted pea____ and chip____ for tea.

9. Add 'an' or 'a' to the nouns in these questions.

a. What mini beast has _____ shell on its back?

b. What does ____ hen lay?

c. Where does _____ acorn come from?

d. What is _____ baby cat called?

10. Add 'an' or 'a' to the noun answers

_____ snail.

_____ egg.

_____ oak tree.

_____ kitten.

Periodic Assessment test 1 - Pronouns

Name: _____

Date: _____

Class: _____

Level: _____

1. Circle these pronouns in the sentences.

I	me	my	you	your
she	her	he	him	his

a. I like fish and chips.

b. Nan thinks my picture is great

c. Do you need me?

d. The book is in your bag.

e. She gave him a present

f. He loved his new tie.

g. Her present was a tin of beans.

2. Add in the missing pronouns.

a. Mia is stuck in the mud. _____ needs a pull.

b. Can I see _____ new marble?

c. The queen opened _____ box.

d. The king wanted _____ bath.

3. Write a short sentence using one of these pronouns.

I   my   she   he

_____

4. Circle these pronouns in the sentences.

we	us	our	your
them	their	they	

a. Joe and I went to the park. We played football.

b. You can't catch us!

c. This is our new house.

d. "We love your UFO," they said to the aliens

e. The hens laid their eggs.

f. The sweets were gone. Who had eaten them?

5. Add in the missing pronouns.

a. Can we go to the shops?

b. This is our tent.

c. Their door is red and blue.

d. Jack and Jill fell and the bucket fell behind them.

6. Write a short sentence using one of these pronouns.

We   our   they

_____

Periodic Assessment test 2 – Pronouns

Name: _____

Date: _____

Class: _____

Level: _____

1. Circle these pronouns in the sentences.

I	me	my	you	your
she	her	he	him	his

a. Lily cooked a cake. She put icing on top.

b. Ben has asked me over to play.

c. Have you seen my yo-yo?

d. I have found your book.

e. Nan is taking her dog to the vets.

f. The king is cross. He wants to take his water wings with him.

2. Change the underlined words into a pronoun. Rewrite the sentence with the pronoun on the lines.

Mrs Shaw put Mrs Shaw's flowers in a vase.

_____

The cowboy threw the cowboy's rope over the cow.

_____

The queen was happy. The queen has found her crown.

_____

My name is Max. Max like to row boats.

_____

3. Put the missing pronouns into the spaces using the pronouns below.

we	us	our	your
them	their	they	

My class and I went on a school trip to the seaside. _____ built lots of sandcastles on

the beach. Some of _____ had flags on top. _____ teacher gave _____ the

prize for the best sandcastle. "_____ castle is very good," she said to _____.

The rest of the class clapped _____ hands.

4. Change the underlined words into a pronoun. Rewrite the sentence with the pronoun on the lines.

Jo and I like ice skating. Jo and I like going fast around the rink.

_____

The knight s chased the dragons but the knights lost the dragons.

_____

My brother and I are going to the pantomime. Would you like to come with my brother and me?

_____

5. Write one sentence with one of these pronouns: our   we   they.

_____

Periodic Assessment test 1 – Verbs

Name: _____

Date: _____

Class: _____

Level: _____

1. Some of these words are not action verbs. Circle the odd ones out.

   a. jump   giant   run   skip

   b. hop   read   cat   drink

   c. walk   draw catch cup

2. Underline the verbs in the sentences.

   a. Luke likes to ride his bike.

   b. Look at the rabbit hop!

   c. Fish swim in the sea.

   d. I am going to bounce my ball.

3. Draw lines to match the saying verbs with the right pictures.

   cry   laugh   whisper   shout   roar

4. Add the missing saying verbs into the sentences.

   call   shouted   cried   asked

   a. "I have lost my mum," _____ the little boy.

   b. "Who has taken my gold harp?" _____ the giant.

   c. Jess _____ the teacher if she could go out.

   d. I will _____ you after tea.

5. Make these verbs past tense by adding ed or d.

wash	washed
cook	_____
pull	_____
dance	danced
like	_____
bake	_____

6. Add ed or d to the verbs in sentences.

a. The farmer pull_____ out the large turnip.

b. The farmer's wife cook_____ the turnip.

c. The goat chase_____ the boy.

d. The worm wiggle_____ under a leaf.

7. Make these verbs present tense by add ing.

call	calling
read	_____
look	_____
make	making
ride	_____
wave	_____

8. Add ing to the verbs in sentences.

a. Sam and I are playing football.

b. My dad is cooking lunch today.

c. Ella loves riding her new bike.

d. I am writing a letter to my auntie.

9. Colour in each pair of irregular verbs with a different colour.

dig	see	make	fall
made	fell	dug	saw

Periodic Assessment test 2 – Verbs

Name: _____

Date: _____

Class: _____

Level: _____

1. Underline the action verbs in the sentences.

    a. I am going to watch TV later.

    b. Harry went to the tower to ring the bell.

    c. The children had a swim in the sea.

    d. The monkey can swing from tree to tree.

2. Put an action verb in the spaces.

    a. Callum used the bat to _____ the ball.

    b. The girl used her paint brushes to _____ a picture.

    c. Jack and Jill want to _____ down the hill.

    d. The dog began to _____ and _____ his tail.

3. Underline the saying verbs.

    a. Kelly asked her mum for a biscuit.

    b. The old man grumbled at the dropped litter.

    c. "Watch out!" shouted Liam.

    d. "Stop tickling me," giggled Holly.

4. Choose saying verbs to replace the word 'said'.

    cried   asked   whispered

    a. "I think I have broken my arm," said Poppy._____

    b. "This is the secret code," said the spy. _____

    c. "Have you seen my socks?" said Joe. _____

5. Rewrite these verbs into past tense by adding ed or d

bounce _____   chew _____   push _____

share _____   sail_____   wave _____

6. Write two sentences using these past tense verbs.
rained   cooked

_____

_____

7. Rewrite these verbs into present tense by adding ing.

read_____   laugh_____   bake_____

ring_____   love_____   slide_____

8. Add in the missing present tense verbs to the sentences.

At the Zoo, the lions are roar_____ at the visitors.

The snake is hiss_____ at a boy.

The monkeys are jump_____ up and down.

The kangaroos are bounce _____ around.

9. Use different coloured pencils to colour in each pair of irregular verbs with a different colour. What is the shape?

			came	fall			
			go	tell			
saw	did	told	gave	win	sold	got	fell
		won	sit	get	said		
		sell	say	sat	went		
		come			do		
		see			give		

Periodic Assessment test 1 - Adjectives

Name: _____

Date: _____

Class: _____

Level: _____

1. On of these words is not an adjective (a describing word). Circle the odd one out.

a. big   cold   cow   tall

b. small   hot   wet   ball

c. dry   leg   white   high

2. Underline the five adjectives in the sentences. Draw a picture of it.

The land looked cold. The trees were white with snow. The pond was very icy. A big snowman looked very happy.

3. Look at the picture of the clown. Put in the adjectives from below in the sentences to show what he looks like.

spotty

curly

big

round

The clown has a _____ nose.

His hair has _____ hair.

He has a _____ mouth.

He has a _____ hat.

4. Draw a line to match a word with its opposite word.

hot	small
wet	sad
happy	cold
big	dry

5. Circle the words that are odd one out in the sentences.

a. big   large   huge   little

b. small   short   happy   tiny

c. ill   rich   unwell   sick

6. Put a circle round the word that means the same as the underlined word

a. The giant was very cross. (angry   sad   happy)

b. The elf was very small. (tall, ugly, little.)

c. The train was very quick. (quick, slow, soft)

Periodic Assessment test 2 - Adjectives

Name: _____

Date: _____

Class: _____

Level: _____

1. Add in adjectives to complete the sentences.

haunted   steep   slimy   scary   blue   wet

The rocks were _____ and _____.

From the top of the _____ hill, Ben could see the _____ sea.

The _____ castle was very _____.

2. Circle the adjectives you would like to use to describe a planet.

The rocket touched down on the rocky / grassy ground. Two orange / purple suns shone their

hot / cold rays onto the planet. A dusty / foggy track led to a large / small lake. Next to it was a

lovely / scary looking alien city.

3. Use some of these adjectives to write three sentences describing an alien.
   Draw a picture of it in the box.

friendly	slimy	scary	soft	scaly	two	three
four	googly	fat	tall	short	thin	
large	small	spotty	shy	loud	quiet	hairy

_____

_____

_____

4. Draw a line to match the word to its antonym (opposite) word.

a. fast   well

b. light   rich

c. dirty   slow

d. poor   heavy

e. sick   clean

5. Add in the antonyms to the sentences.

fast   cold   sad   dirty   hot   clean   slow   happy

a. In winter it is _____ but in the summer it is _____.

b. When I got into the bath I was _____ but now I am _____

c. The hare ran very _____ and the tortoise ran very_____

d. Mia was _____ to see her friends but _____ when they left.

6. Draw lines to match the words to the synonyms that mean the same.

tall   small   cold

icy   little   big   tiny   cool   large   high   short   chilly

7. Circle a synonym to make the sentences more interesting.

a. The giant's castle was big. (huge, vast, enormous).

b. The red rose was very pretty. (beautiful, lovely, sweet).

c. Rob's coat was wet. (soaking, damp, soggy).

Periodic Assessment test 1 - Sentences

Name: _____

Date: _____

Class: _____

Level: _____

1. Add the missing capital letter and full stops.

   a. my mum is making a cup of tea

   b. he boy jumped out of the tree

   c. i have lost my ring

2. Use three colour pencils to match the two parts of simple sentences.

The lollipop lady	are going to the fair.
Liam and I	was very cross.
The troll	stopped the cars.

3. Underline the joining words in the sentences.

   a. Molly put the kettle on and she ate some cake.

   b. I can come to tea but I must ask my mum.

   c. I am tired so I will go to bed.

4. Add in a joining word.

and	but	so

I like pasta _____ I do not like rice.

I need new shoes _____ I can play football.

The plates are out _____ the food is cooked.

5. Underline the time words

First I put my boots on.

Then I put my coat on.

Next I put my hat on.

Finally I put my scarf on.

6. Add the time words to the sentences.

Draw pictures to go with each sentence.

First	Then	Next	Finally	Later on

_____I dig a hole.

_____I put the seeds in the hole.

_____I put the earth back.

_____I water the seeds.

_____ the seeds grow into flowers.

7. Underline the position words.

off	on	next	under	behind	above	in front

a. The cup is on the table.

b. The snail is under the leaf.

c. The ball is behind the shed.

d. The book is above the TV.

Periodic Assessment test 2 - Sentences

Name: _____

Date: _____

Class: _____

Level: _____

1. Add capital letters and full stops to show the five sentences in the story.

hetty went to see her auntie for a cup of tea at her auntie's house she saw a bear hiding in the bushes hetty ran inside to tell her auntie they went outside to find it but the bear had gone all they found was a big jar of honey.

2. Number these sentences to show the right order.

She went to England to help nurse people.

After the war she was given medals.

Mary Seacole was born in 1805.

She then went to the Crimean War to nurse soldiers.

As a girl she wanted to be a nurse.

3. Underline a joining word in the sentences.

a. I want to climb the hill but my foot is sore.

b. The mouse nibbled the cheese and then he fell asleep.

c. The car broke down so I walked to school.

4. Add in the correct joining word.

and	but	so	or

I must go _____ I might miss the bus.

I could eat the carrots _____ I could eat the peas.

Davy likes oranges _____ he likes lemons.

I would like to play _____ I have a cold.

5. Underline the time word (time connectives)

a. First the explorer jumped out of bed.

b. Then he slid down the stairs.

c. Next he climbed onto the table.

d. Finally he had his breakfast.

6. Add in the missing time words (time connectives). Draw pictures to go with each sentence.

First	Then	Next	Finally	Later on

_____ we put on our coats and boots.	
_____we walked to the bonfire.	
_____ we watched the bonfire.	
_____we watched the fireworks.	
_____we had hot soup and rolls.	

7. Underline the prepositions.

a. The car is next to a lorry.

b. The fire-fighter is on a tall ladder.

c. My shoes are under the bed.

d. The rabbit is hiding behind the sofa.

e. The UFO is flying above us.

f. The runner is in front of the other runners.

8. Write sentences about where four objects are in your classroom using some of these prepositions.

on	next	under	behind	above	in front of

_____

_____

_____

_____

Periodic Assessment test 1- Punctuation

Name: _____

Date: _____

Class: _____

Level: _____

1. Add on the question marks to the questions.

    a. What is your name

    b. How old are you

    c. Where do you live

    d. Who is your best friend

    e. When were you born

2. Draw a line to match the answer to the questions. Underline the questions words in the questions.

<u>What</u> is a baby lion called?	My birthday is in May.
How many legs has a spider?	An apple is green.
Where is Big Ben?	A baby lion is called a cub.
Who is Mary Seacole?	A spider has eight legs.
When is your birthday?	Big Ben is in London.
Which is green, a carrot or apple?	Mary Seacole was a nurse.

3. Add commas to the list.

For my birthday I got a robot socks paints a book a bike and a CD.

4. Make a list out of these words and add in comma

monkey   snake   lion   goat   and a hippo.

At the zoo I saw _____

_____

_____

5. Match the speech bubbles to the pictures

6. Put speech marks into the sentences. "_"

a. ____ Who had my hairy toe? _____ yelled the monster.

b. ____ Tea time, _____ called mum.

c. _____ Watch out! _____ shouted the man.

Periodic Assessment test 2- Punctuation

Name: _____

Date: _____

Class: _____

Level: _____

1. Write the questions to these answers.

_____

A baby horse is called a foal.

_____

I am seven years old.

_____

This egg was laid by a dinosaur.

_____

I would like to eat curry and rice.

2. Complete theses questions with your own words. Underline the question words.

a. Where is the _____

b. Who is your _____

c. When can you _____

d. How does a _____

e. What is a _____

f. Which games do you _____

3. Add commas to this list.

When I went to the party dressed as an explorer I wore heavy boots   waterproof trousers   a coat
a warm hat   a stripy scarf and a pair of gloves.

4. Make a list using some of these words.

brushes   glue   paint   scissors   pencils   paper

In the art cupboard there are _____

_____

5. Add in the speech marks to the speaking words.

_____ Get out of my way! _____ shouted the robber.

_____ Can I tell you a secret? _____ whispered the ghost.

_____ I wish I could have a toffee apple, _____ sighed Tom.

6. Rewrite these sentences into speech and add pictures with them.

This pizza is yummy!   Do you like my new spotty boots?

_____   _____

Transitional Assessment Test 1

Name: _____

Date: _____

Class: _____

Level: _____

Common nouns
Circle the words that are nouns.

car	funny	pirate	house	run	ball
clown	school	cow	sad	cry	lion

Proper nouns
Give the proper nouns in the sentences a capital letter.

a. My teacher is called mrs gaskin.

b. I went to devon for my holiday.

c. Tomorrow is Monday.

d. My brother is called Leo.

Common nouns and proper nouns
Underline the proper nouns in the sentences. Circle the common nouns in the sentences.

a. We stayed in a caravan at Sunny Days Park.

b. My uncle lives in Canada.

c. The bus stops at the High Street.

d. I bought a hat at Hatters.

Compound nouns
Write the three compound nouns beginning with 'foot.'

_____

_____

_____

Plural nouns ending with 's'
Turn these nouns into plurals. Use one to write a short sentence.

elephant____   drum_____   hut_____   lion_____

_____

Articles: 'an' or 'a'
Add 'an' or 'a' in the missing spaces.

a. The rabbit hopped into _____ hole.

b. Have you got _____ umbrella?

c. _____ octopus has eight legs.

d. The cat is in _____ tree.

Singular pronouns

I	my	you	your
she	he	him	his

Circle the pronouns in the sentences.

a. This is my best friend, Lulu.

b. She is so funny.

c. Your mum has cooked me a cake.

d. Harvey fell on his knees.

e. He did not want him to go.

f. I hope you can come to my party.

Plural Pronouns

we	they	our
them	their	

Underline the pronouns in the sentences.

a. We are going to the circus.

b. Some people were in our seats.

c. Their seats were in another row.

d. They got up and moved to them.

Action verbs
Add the action verbs into the missing spaces.

jump   push   cut   sing.

a. Tim _____ the paper up.

b. Megan likes to _____ songs.

c. Dad had to _____ the car.

d. Let's _____ on my bed.

Saying verbs
Underline the saying verbs.

a. "Can I have an ice-cream?" asked Millie.

b. Jonas yelled at Bella.

c. "I'm tired," yawned the elf.

Past tense verbs ending in ed
Turn these into verbs into past tense using ed or d.

play _____   dance_____

Use the verbs to write two short sentences.

_____

_____

Present tense verbs ending in ing
Rewrite these verbs into present tense using ing.

help _____   save _____

Use the ing verbs to write two short sentences.

_____

_____

Irregular verbs
Draw a line to match the verbs.

see
fall
run

fell
ran
saw

End the sentences in your own words.

a. I can see _____

b. I saw _____

Descriptive adjectives
Write the adjectives next to the right nouns.

cold   hot   dry   blue   rocky

_ _ _ _ sea   _ _ _ _ snow   _ _ _ sun   _ _ _ _ _ hills   _ _ _ desert.

Descriptive adjectives.
Use some of the adjectives to fill in the sentences about this superhero.

long   short   spotty

spiky   funny   great   silly

She is wearing a _____ skirt.

She has _____ boots.

Her hair is _____.

I think she is _____.

Antonyms
Match the opposites to these words.

Wet   hard

Poor   dry

Soft   cold

Hot   rich

Synonyms.
Use a red pencil to colour in the words that mean tall.
Use a blue pencil to colour in the words that mean small.

big	little	tiny
short	high	big

Simple sentences.
Write the mixed up words in the right order.

put kettle on. the Polly

_____

Compound sentences
Put in the right joining words.

and   but

The cat sat in the tree _____ it could not get down.

Katy took her key _____ she opened the door.

Time words (Time connectives)
Underline the time words.

First I beat the eggs.

Then I put the bread in the eggs.

Next I fry the bread.

Finally it is cooked.

Prepositions

| on | next | under | behind |

Look at the picture. Add in the missing prepositions.

The cup is _____ the table.

The ball is _____ the bed.

The toy car is _____ to the robot.

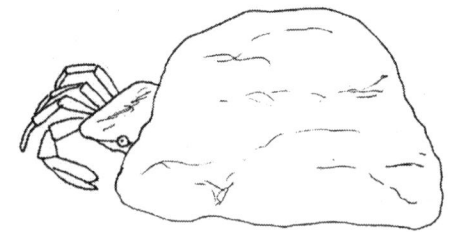

The crab is _____ the rock.

Questions
Add question marks to these questions.

a. Where is the park

b. Who is going to pick up the bean bags

c. How do you make a cup of tea

d. Why did the hen cross the road

Commas in a list
Add commas into the two lists.

In my bedroom there is a bed a rug books   a toy box   a lamp and my teddy.

At the seaside I saw a crab   a seagull a sandcastle a shell and seaweed.

Speech marks.
Add in the speech marks to the speaking words.

____Come down Jack! _____ called out his mum.

_____ I wish I could go to the ball, _____ sighed Cinderella.

Transitional Assessment test 2

Name: _____

Date: _____

Class: _____

Level: _____

Common nouns
Write a sentence about each common noun.

octopus   school   fire-fighter   hat

_____

_____

_____

_____

Proper nouns
There is something wrong with the proper nouns in these sentences.
Re-write them correctly in the spaces.

Have you seen tom (_____)? We need to go to the cinema to see toy story (_____

_____). Afterwards we are going to eat at pizza power (_____).

Common nouns and proper nouns
Write the proper noun answers to the common nouns in the box below.

My name	
The town or village where I live.	
Month I was born.	
My favourite day of the week.	
My favourite book	
A country I would like to visit.	

Compound nouns
Add nouns to the spaces to make compound nouns.

a. hand _____   b. arm-_____

c. butter_____   d. ear _____

e. knee_____   f. key _____

Plural nouns
Rewrite these sentences using plural nouns.

Jack ran down the road to buy some sticky doughnut_____. In the bakery he also bought four fairy

cake_____, three jam tart_____ and six cheese straw_____. The baker wanted ten gold

coin____ but Jack only had two magic bean_____.

Articles - 'an' or 'a'
Add 'an' or 'a' to these nouns.

_____ astronaut   _____ dragon   _____ island

Write sentences using each one.

a. _____

b. _____

c. _____

Singular pronouns

I	me	my	you	your
she	her	he	him	his

Put in the missing pronouns.

Chloe went into lunch with _____ class. "Can _____ sit with _____? "asked Jacob. Jacob took

out _____ lunch. "_____ mum has given _____ a lot of food," he said. "What have you got?" Chloe

looked at _____. "Worms!" _____ laughed.

Plural Pronouns

we	us	our
them	their	they

Underline the pronouns in the sentences.

Joe and I heard a bang. We looked out of our window. Aliens had landed in our garden. We

gave them a cup of tea. Then they went back to their UFOs and zoomed off.

Action verbs
Write sentences using these action verbs.

clap   juggle   paddle

_____

_____

_____

Saying verbs
Write three sentences using three of these saying verbs.

asked   begged   cried   moaned   shouted   laughed   whispered   yawned   sighed

_____

_____

_____

Past tense verbs ending in 'ed' or 'd'
Turn the verbs into past tense verbs.

a. Billy bounce_____ up and down on the trampoline.

b. Francis Drake sail_____ around the world.

c. Leah looked at the picture and giggle_____.

d. Pirate Pip slowly turn_____ the key to the treasure chest.

Present tense verbs ending in ing
Rewrite the verbs into present tense verbs adding ing.

ride _____   ring _____

hide _____   skate_____

Use two of the present tense verbs to write two sentences.

_____

_____

Present tense or past tense verbs
Use a red pencil to colour in the sentences which are in past tense.
Use a blue pencil to colour in the sentences which are in present tense.

| I am hiding under the bed | We laughed at the clown. | Mum is baking a cake. |
| Viv has painted the gate. | I jumped into a puddle. | The dog barked at the cat. |

Irregular verbs
Add in the correct irregular verbs to the sentences.

dig   dug   give   gave   took   take

a. The builder is going to _____ a hole in the road.

b. The pirate _____ up a treasure chest.

c. I am going to _____ my mum a hug.

d. Emma _____ Jacob a new model car.

e. Our teacher is going to _____ us swimming.

f. I _____ my computer game with me.

Descriptive adjectives
Add adjectives to end the sentences.

The beach was very _____

The grass was very _____

The sun was very _____

The snow was very _____

Descriptive adjectives
Write a description of a story book character using some e of these adjectives.

| happy   sad   large   tall   small   little   kind   nasty   ugly   pretty |
| brave   scary   shy   quiet   noisy   funny   angry   clever   stupid |

_____

_____

_____

_____

Antonyms
Write the antonyms (opposites) to the words in the box.

happy	
dirty	
big	
fat	
loud	
soft	
wet	
hot	
poor	

Synonyms
Write two synonyms for each of these words below.

cold = _____

hot = _____

Simple sentences
Write the mixed up words in the right order.

shoemaker The man. a poor very was

_____

fireworks the We sky. the sparkle in

_____

Write your own sentence about Bonfire Night.

_____

_____

Compound sentence
Add in the missing joining words of the compound sentences.

and	but	or	so

a. Josh kicked the ball _____ it went in the goal.

b. I can go to the park _____ I can play in the garden.

c. Harry came to see his Gran _____ the lift was broken.

d. The book fell on the floor _____ Lily picked it up.

Time connectives
Complete the sentences that start with time connectives to describe your day.

First _____

_____

Then _____

_____

Next _____

_____

Finally _____

_____

Preposition
Use these prepositions to explain where the objects are.

on	next	under	behind

cup	plate	kettle	chair

_____

_____

_____

_____

Questions
Write the questions to the animal answers.

_____

Kangaroos come from Australia.

_____

The tallest animal is the giraffe.

_____

The snail has a shell for a home.

_____

The fastest animal in the world is the cheetah.

Commas in a list
Add commas to the list.

You can have strawberry   chocolate   vanilla lemon   coconut or cherry ice cream.

Write a list of your five favourite foods.

_____

_____

Speech marks
Rewrite these sentences adding in the speech marks.

I want my mummy cried the prince.   Look at that rocket firework said Mia

I'm hungry roared the lion.

_____

_____

_____

Assessment Charts
Writing Assessment chart

Grammar subject	Assessment Focus (AFs) Level 1	Assessment Focus (AFs) Level 2
Common nouns	**AF7:** mostly simple vocabulary	**AF7:** some adventurous wrd choices
Proper nouns	**AF6:** some awareness of use of full stops and capital letters, e.g. beginning/end of sentence	**AF6:** sentence demarcation with capital letters and full stops usually accurate
Compound nouns	**AF1:** some descriptive language, e.g. colour, size, simple emotion	**AF1:** some apt word choices create interest
Plural nouns -s	**AF7:** mostly simple vocabulary	**AF7:** some adventurous wrd choices
Articles	**AF7:** mostly simple vocabulary	**AF7:** some adventurous wrd choices
Singular pronouns	**AF4:** simple connections between ideas, events, e.g. repeated nouns, pronouns relate to main idea	**AF4:** ideas in sections grouped by content, some linking by simple pronouns
Plural pronouns	**AF4:** simple connections between ideas, events, e.g. repeated nouns, pronouns relate to main idea	**AF4:** ideas in sections grouped by content, some linking by simple pronouns **AF8:** inflected endings, e.g. past tense, plurals, adverbs
Action verbs	**AF7:** mostly simple vocabulary	**AF7:** some adventurous wrd choices
Saying verbs	**AF1:** some descriptive language, e.g. colour, size, simple emotion	**AF1:** some apt word choices create interest
Past tense verbs -ed	**AF8:** usually correct spelling of simple high-frequency words	**AF5:** past and present tense generally consistent **AF8:** inflected endings, e.g. past tense, plurals, adverbs
Present tense verbs -ing	**AF8:** usually correct spelling of simple high-frequency words	**AF5:** past and present tense generally consistent **AF8:** inflected endings, e.g. past tense, plurals, adverbs
Irregular verbs	**AF8:** usually correct spelling of simple high-frequency words	**AF8** inflected endings, e.g. past tense, plurals, adverbs
Descriptive adjectives 1	**AF1:** some descriptive language, e.g. colour, size, simple emotion	**AF1:** some apt word choices create interest
Descriptive adjectives 2	**AF1:** some descriptive language, e.g. colour, size, simple emotion	**AF1:** some apt word choices create interest
Antonyms	**AF1:** some descriptive language, e.g. colour, size, simple emotion	**AF1:** some apt word choices create interest **AF7:** some adventurous word choices, e.g. opportune use of new vocabulary
Synonyms	**AF1:** some descriptive language, e.g. colour, size, simple emotion	**AF1:** some apt word choices create interest. **AF7:** some adventurous word choices, e.g. opportune use of new vocabulary
Simple sentences	**AF5:** reliance on simple phrases and clauses **AF6:** some awareness of use of full stops and capital letters, e.g. beginning/end of sentence.	**AF5::** clause structure mostly grammatically correct **AF6:** sentence demarcation with capital letters and full stops usually accurate
Compound sentences	**AF5:** some sentence-like structures formed by chaining clauses together, e.g. series of ideas joined by repeated use of 'and'	**AF5:** mainly simple sentences with and used to connect clauses
Time connectives	**AF5:** reliance on simple phrases and clauses **AF3:** events/ideas sometimes in appropriate order, e.g. actions listed in time sequence, items numbered	**AF5:** mainly simple sentences with and used to connect clauses **AF3:** some basic sequencing of ideas or material, e.g. time-related words or phrases, line breaks, headings, numbers

Grammar subject	Assessment Focus (AFs) Level 1	Assessment Focus (AFs) Level 2
Prepositions	**AF5:** reliance on simple phrases and clauses	**AF5:** mainly simple sentences with and used to connect clauses
Questions	**AF1:** basic information and ideas conveyed through appropriate word choice, e.g. relate to topic	**AF6:** some accurate use of question and exclamation marks, and commas in lists **AF1:** brief comments, questions about events or actions suggest viewpoint
Commas	**AF2:** some indication of basic purpose, particular form or awareness of reader, e.g. story, label, message	**AF6:** some accurate use of question and exclamation marks, and commas in lists
Speech marks	**AF2:** some indication of basic purpose, particular form or awareness of reader, e.g. story, label, message	**AF7:** simple, often speech-like vocabulary conveys relevant meanings **AF2:** some appropriate features of the given form used

Reading Assessment chart

Grammar subject	Assessment Focus (AFs) Level 1	Assessment Focus (AFs) Level 2
Common nouns	**AF1:** decode familiar and some unfamiliar words using blending as the prime approach	**AF1:** unfamiliar words decoded using appropriate strategies, e.g. blending sounds
Proper nouns	**AF4:** some awareness of meaning of simple text features, e.g. font style, labels, titles	**AF4:** use of features of organisation, e.g. beginning and ending of story, types of punctuation
Compound nouns	**AF5:** comments on obvious features of language, e.g. rhymes and refrains, significant words and phrases	**AF5:** some effective language choices noted, e.g. '"slimy" is a good word there'
Plural nouns -s	**AF1:** decode familiar and some unfamiliar words using blending as the prime approach	**AF1:** unfamiliar words decoded using appropriate strategies, e.g. blending sounds
Articles	**AF5:** features of language, e.g. rhymes and refrains, significant words and phrases	**AF5:** some familiar patterns of language identified, e.g. once upon a time; first, next, last
Singular pronouns	**AF5:** features of language, e.g. rhymes and refrains, significant words and phrases	**AF5:** some familiar patterns of language identified, e.g. once upon a time; first, next, last
Plural pronouns	**AF5:** features of language, e.g. rhymes and refrains, significant words and phrases	**AF5:** some familiar patterns of language identified, e.g. once upon a time; first, next, last
Action verbs	**AF1:** decode familiar and some unfamiliar words using blending as the prime approach	**AF1:** unfamiliar words decoded using appropriate strategies, e.g. blending sounds
Saying verbs	**AF3:** reasonable inference at a basic level, e.g. identifying who is speaking in a story	**AF3:** simple, plausible inference about events and information, using evidence from text, e.g. how a character is feeling
Past tense verbs -ed	**AF1:** decode familiar and some unfamiliar words using blending as the prime approach	**AF1:** unfamiliar words decoded using appropriate strategies, e.g. blending sounds
Present tense verbs -ing	**AF1:** decode familiar and some unfamiliar words using blending as the prime approach	**AF1:** unfamiliar words decoded using appropriate strategies, e.g. blending sounds
Irregular verbs	**AF1:** decode familiar and some unfamiliar words using blending as the prime approach	**AF1:** unfamiliar words decoded using appropriate strategies, e.g. blending sounds
Descriptive adjectives 1	**AF5:** comments on obvious features of language, e.g. rhymes and refrains, significant words and phrases	**AF5:** some effective language choices noted, e.g. '"slimy" is a good word there'
Descriptive adjectives 2	**AF5:** comments on obvious features of language, e.g. rhymes and refrains, significant words and phrases	**AF5:** some effective language choices noted, e.g. '"slimy" is a good word there'
Antonyms	**AF5:** comments on obvious features of language, e.g. rhymes and refrains, significant words and phrases	**AF5:** some effective language choices noted, e.g. '"slimy" is a good word there'
Synonyms	**AF5:** comments on obvious features of language, e.g. rhymes and refrains, significant words and phrases	**AF5:** some effective language choices noted, e.g. '"slimy" is a good word there'
Simple sentences	**AF1:** some awareness of punctuation marks, e.g. pausing at full stops	**AF1:** some fluency and expression, e.g. taking account of punctuation, speech marks
Compound sentences	**AF5:** features of language, e.g. rhymes and refrains, significant words and phrases	**AF5:** some familiar patterns of language identified, e.g. once upon a time; first, next, last
Time connectives	**AF5:** features of language, e.g. rhymes and refrains, significant words and phrases	**AF5:** some familiar patterns of language identified, e.g. once upon a time; first, next, last
Prepositions	**AF5:** features of language, e.g. rhymes and refrains, significant words and phrases	**AF5:** some familiar patterns of language identified, e.g. once upon a time; first, next, last

Grammar subject	Assessment Focus (AFs) Level 1	Assessment Focus (AFs) Level 2
Questions	**AF1:** some awareness of punctuation marks, e.g. pausing at full stops **AF3:** comments/questions about meaning of parts of text, e.g. details of illustrations diagrams, changes in font style	**AF1:** some fluency and expression, e.g. taking account of punctuation, speech marks **AF3:** simple, plausible inference about events and information, using evidence from text, e.g. how a character is feeling, what makes a plant grow
Commas	**AF1:** some awareness of punctuation marks, e.g. pausing at full stops	**AF1:** some fluency and expression, e.g. taking account of punctuation, speech marks
Speech marks	**AF1:** some awareness of punctuation marks, e.g. pausing at full stops **AF3:** reasonable inference at a basic level, e.g. identifying who is speaking in a story	**AF1:** some fluency and expression, e.g. taking account of punctuation, speech marks **AF3:** simple, plausible inference about events and information, using evidence from text, e.g. how a character is feeling, what makes a plant grow

Notes

Notes